i never dreamed you'd leave in summer

A Mother's Journey from Mourning to Morning

Crystal P. Willingham

I Never Dreamed You'd Leave in Summer

Copyright © 2019 by Crystal P. Willingham.

All rights reserved. Printed in the United States of America. No part of this book may be used or reproduced in any manner whatsoever without written permission except in the case of brief quotations em- bodied in critical articles or reviews.

This book is a work of fiction. Names, characters, businesses, organiza- tions, places, events and incidents either are the product of the author's imagination or are used fictitiously. Any resemblance to actual persons, living or dead, events, or locales is entirely coincidental.

For information contact :

www.iamclearascrystal.com

Published by :

Relentless Publishing House, LLC

Book and Cover design by Ash Ahern

ISBN: 9781948829342

First Edition: August 2019

10 9 8 7 6 5 4 3 2 1

TABLE OF CONTENTS

Introduction 1
Chapter 1: What Happened? 21
Chapter 2: Now What? 67
Chapter 3: Mourning & Grieving 85
Chapter 4: Triggers & Trauma 99
Chapter 5: The Bigger Picture 119
Chapter 6: What Next 135
Chapter 7: Trauma 145
About the Author
Acknowledgements

Introduction

Losing a child is devastating. The day little Symara Phylesha-Briann Smith was born, I never imagined that I would lose her. I never contemplated losing any of my children. So, do we ever contemplate that at first glance or when we first hold them in our arms? Every child I gave birth to I held them in my arms and thought about their future. Not once did I ever entertain the thought that their future would be short lived. It's not something you normally think about on the day of your child's birth, unless perhaps there is a terminal diagnosis and an expectation that the baby will not live long afterward. I was thinking about diapers, formula, sleep patterns, siblings, grandchildren, and graduation from college. As a parent, you can always look to the future when it comes to your children but you seldom, if ever, plan for them to die. I remember when her father took out the life insurance policy for all of us. When the children turned 18, we planned to have them cash it in for college or maybe for their first car. We never actually planned to use those funds for death.

    I had been waiting over the last few years for the right time to write this story. I would occasionally sit down and begin writing; then I would be overcome by a whirlwind of thoughts and emotions. Sometimes these writing sessions turned into full-fledged conversations with God. There were times I would stop writing just to think about what I was feeling and why. I often wondered, after a few years of trying to heal from one of the most tragic moments of my life, if I would ever be able to breathe and live normally again. The answer is yes... and no. It was simple to me. I would breathe again, but I had to find a new normal, a new breath, and learn to live in the best way possible.

It took a little bit of time to come to this conclusion, as it was hard for me to believe that I could obtain this level of peace about everything. I had heard a few rumors; some people felt I deserved jail time for the accident I caused. On some level - I agreed, and, since I was not prosecuted, I figured I would punish myself. I felt, at times, I did not even deserve to draw breath again because my little girl died. I never told anyone about all my feelings, but I continually sabotaged my future and doubted the value of my life in its entirety. This is how I lived for a very long time. I didn't need the condemnation of public opinion or even the negative opinions of family and friends. I was pretty good at silently punishing myself. I felt abandoned by many people even though some empathized with my pain and reached out to me. I couldn't seem to get past the "fault line". You know, that line where you perpetually blame and punish yourself for the things that have gone wrong in your life? I dismissed the thought that what happened to Symara was an accident and I chose to shoulder all the blame internally.

  I played the role of a "good", resilient woman because that is all I knew to do. I learned from a very young age that when something bad or sad happens, I am supposed to get up and bounce back. I'm not quite sure if this behavior was taught or caught, but all the same I learned it at a very young age. Further, I had convinced myself that it doesn't matter what happens, no one will hear you or could possibly understand you, So - you will just have to get back up on your own and move ahead. To sum it all up, I was on my own. I hadn't publicly shared the nights I lay wide-awake and asking God to end my life. The only people who knew about these emotions were my other children, Symara's father. During this time, my husband Marlon helped me understand grief, depression, and pain. He came into my life like a breath of fresh air and new glasses. I had moments of depression, but I didn't succumb to it wholly. I knew better than to allow that to happen. I needed to be present for my children to make sure they got through better than me somehow.

After my husband Marlon entered my life, my taste of fresh air, I made a decision that would change my life and chart the course of my happiness. I decided I would no longer be the saboteur of my own life and continue to live inside of an emotional prison (I often described my life as a prison that I had to fight to get out of every single day). One day, I just got up and said, "That's enough prison time". That was the day I revisited the cross and realized once again the true story of Christ's suffering for all of us. He died for every sin, weight, and painful situation of life. He even wept for Lazurus his friend although he knew he was about to raise him from the dead, he knew that pain. I began to break out of the prison that I had voluntarily walked into every single day of my life since August 13, 2009. That was the day I was set free and never looked back. Realistically, her death still affects me, and I often cry for the empty space I feel in my life as a mother. The void that was once there has been filled with the peace and presence of God, the love of my life, and the continued growth of my family and friends.

Grieving is an inevitable journey in life. You will experience it and you will see it differently with each kind of loss. Each person you grieve elicits their own, unique journey of responses. When you grieve, it's almost as if your life takes a detour - and you are forced to take that alternate route, whether you want to or not. You have to reroute your thinking, actions, and living habits when you are experiencing the loss of someone you love dearly. You cannot avoid it. You cannot change it. However, you cannot let death stop you from living. You just have to stop, mourn and reroute, and your ultimate destination is not supposed to change.

You may have to change *how* you live, but you *must keep living*. If you lose a spouse, you will have to sleep alone. If you lose a best friend, you will have to get used to not texting, calling, or writing letters. If you lose a parent, you'll have to hold tight to the memories of growing up. You must create a new normal within your life so that you can keep moving forward. There is no way around it. You cannot avoid it. Death is the inevitable, emotional, strand of our life span we wish we could extract. We know it is coming eventually, but whenever it happens, we don't "seem" to be prepared. Especially for those sudden exits from life, you know when your loved one is here today and gone tomorrow? Do you know what I mean? When your child, husband, or parent leaves the house for school, work, or to go the cleaners and the police knock on your door and tell you that your loved one has just passed away. Sudden deaths suck you into a whirlwind of questions that never find answers. You try to remember the details of your last conversation – down to the last word, that each of you spoke. What were they wearing? Did you say you loved them? Did you argue, or did you kiss?

What about when your loved one is terminally ill, and you think you're prepared until they take their last breath? You may find yourself asking God to give you more time, to let them stay a little longer because either you're not ready or you know how deeply you'll miss them. It is such a conundrum: you know that their suffering has finally ended and gloriously you rejoice for them while you simultaneously weep because they will now be absent from your life. This is one part of the journey that will either make you stronger or find and exacerbate any weaknesses you may have. The pain of a loss can be intense, numbing, and paralytic, sometimes all at the same time and other times at different intervals.

Now, I have spent just a few moments telling you how unprepared you are for death, but to be honest you have been prepared all along. From the moment you can comprehend living, you begin preparing for death, but in a very uncertain way. You know it is coming and you know it must happen, but what we do is live until that day arrives, without acknowledging or preparing for the inevitable deaths we will encounter. We do this on life's autopilot without thinking about it and without taking a break, we live on. We go to school, find our spiritual roots, get married, start families, build careers, and we keep living. We just keep living until death happens. When it does, we are forced to stop, acknowledge it, and figure out what to do from there, to somehow find a way to move forward. Time with God, family, and friends help you do just that. Isolation is never the solution to this life change.

You may spend some time alone, but never isolate yourself from the ones who are there to hold you up, dry your tears, cook your food, and just listen. Not everyone has those kinds of people in their lives so if you know someone who is grieving take responsibility to be there for them. Travel to see them if you have to but just be there.

In the book of Genesis, we read the story of creation. In the beginning, God said what He wanted. He said let there be light, land, vegetation, animals, and mankind. Another key thing He said was, "...it is not good for man to be alone." From that point on He establishes relationships and the need for us to have them. No matter what personality traits you have, how independent you may think you are, you still cannot live your life without the interaction of another human's existence. It happens no matter what. I am an introvert -- at least that is how I think of myself. Crowds of people who are total strangers scare me sometimes, yet if you put me into a room

I Never Dreamed You'd Leave in Summer

with them and tell me to speak, I can. I can interact, tell jokes, look a person in the eye and touch their soul. I can hang out, make everyone feel comfortable and take selfies, but when I am done - I am done. I almost run and must return to my place of peace and solace. It doesn't matter that I like being alone; I cannot fulfill my purpose without relationships with people. People help you grow and when you need them to, they help you grieve. Since we know that death is a part of life, we must embrace people and trust our time with them is in God's hands. Acknowledging this truth makes you cherish people more. It leads you to stop wasting time building relationships with people who do not have a purpose in your life. This perspective leads you to appreciate the value of good relationships, to choose them with intention and nurture them correctly. You treat people who mean the world to you very differently. These are the people you have in your life with no ulterior motive but to love them. You hold them closer, talk to them more often, and love them harder. When those cherished people leave your life, the grieving may also be harder, but you take a chance on loving them and embrace them anyway.

      Now, some would ask how God could be so cruel as to let us have children, fall in love, or have relationships with people who are going to die or leave us. It's as though we take death as a personal vendetta that God perpetuates against us. We forget the Bible refers to there being a right time for everything. Some of us become angry with God and blame Him for the passing of our dear ones - as if He just pulled their card with no regard to how those left behind may feel. Here's the ultimate question: If it was you who died suddenly, how do you think those you left behind would feel about your absence? Exactly - there's nothing you can do about it to change how people may feel. The best answer is to just live your life completely and fully patterned after the life of Christ as best you know how. Why? So that when you do leave the world, you will leave your loved ones missing you but with the strength to move on.

One of the greatest and most profound books in the Bible, in my opinion, is the book of Ecclesiastes, and it tells us this, "...there's a time to be born and a time to die." (Eccl 3:2). What an unpretentious but powerful thing to write in a book that would be read by millions. Solomon didn't disregard the gritty human aspect of living. He left no stone unturned when he included his personal philosophical nuggets of wisdom about life of riches and wealth. To me, he was raw and uncut, much like these pages of my life that I am about to share with you. Solomon made it clear about living and dying. If you are born, it is your turn, your time. If you die, it is still your turn. It is also your turn to be here when the inevitable happens and one of your loved ones leaves suddenly.

While writing this book, one song was getting heavy radio play: "I Never Dreamed You'd Leave in Summer" by Stevie Wonder. Although the lyrics refer to the loss of a romantic love, this song really spoke to my heart when I thought of Symara's departure from earth. This is how the name of this book came to me. As I said earlier, I never anticipated on the day she was born that I'd have to say goodbye to her so soon or ever. As a parent, you never plan to bury your children, you plan for the alternate ending. When I look back now, it was as if she was telling me throughout her last few months on Earth she was about to leave us. She asked me questions about death, God, and Heaven, but I never thought she was leaving me. I just figured she was being especially intuitive at her young age. It's funny that sometimes we look at the death of our loved ones as if they decided, willfully, to leave us. There are tragic cases where people have taken their own lives, but even then, I believe they felt they had no other choice. Writing this, I am reminded of my godson who took his life this year. That is a story of loss in another way.

Death is the one life event the pulls most strongly on the emotions of humanity. We value life more than anything. Life and breath - they are more valuable than money, time, and things. If we could only get time back for our loved one to breathe again and tell us one more thing. If only we could laugh at one last joke or participate one more time in our loved one's crazy shenanigans. If we could only kiss them, hold them, and just be near them one more time. If only we could apologize for the last fight, disagreement, or act of revenge. The harsh reality is that wishing for "one more time" will not change the fact that they are gone.

October 26, 2004 was the day Symara was born. Her time of death was 10:26 pm on August 13, 2009 - just four years of living a life that was just a vapor to me. At the time, I wished with all my heart that those days could be longer. I grieved, I mourned, hard. A parent losing a child is not the normal order of things. I didn't come easily to the realization she was gone. I had to find a way to create a new normal without my daughter that cherished and honored my memories of her. Grieving: I had some days where I was way up. Then there were the days when I was way down and depressed; the down days I tried to hide from people. Some days, I could not even bring myself to tell some of my closest friends how despondent I was. Some people didn't understand me, and I lost their friendship. But for what it's worth, I eventually found my peace and oh, what peace it is!

What some people fail to realize is that it's not always healthy, possible or necessary to get back to the "old normal" in order to move on. When we have lost someone, who was a constant in our daily lives it can be easy to trap ourselves

I Never Dreamed You'd Leave in Summer

inside of the pain because we are looking for the old normal to return. You have to let yourself experience the pain of loss, move through it, so you can heal. Let those who love and care about you be there for you. Yes, I had times where I couldn't deal with the pain and I didn't want to be here anymore. It was those people who loved me and whom I love dearly that kept me going. They prayed for me and watched out for me from a distance. I never wanted to take my life, but on bad days, I wouldn't have said no to a permanent exit strategy to leave this life for good. I would often tell God that it would be ok if he would take me out of here. I did eventually realized if I allowed the enemy of humanity, the forces of evil, to use this grief against me, it was just another way for him to win - to kill me, steal and destroy the joys of living for me. I decided to stop suffering and start living. Every day afterwards, I woke up and decided to fight back. I have had more up days than down - at least I would like to believe that. The up days I cherish most because is proved that God's strength is perfected in my human weakness.

    Grief can be that prison that keeps you in and others out. Grief can put you in a place where you may feel you need to control your emotions and actions, so either you cannot feel pain, or you prolong it by trying to ignore it. Grief is that feeling of deep sorrow that can take over your life and keep you trapped in a past you can't change. Grief may have you feeling as if the person who is gone abandoned you, but that's not it at all! One day, long after losing my daughter, I finally woke up and understood what this hard grief was doing to me. I began to realize what I had been missing since that night in August. I didn't have an out of the body, epiphanic moment in time but was saved by LOVE!
LOVE found me through my husband, Marlon, and breathed a second wind into my life. I started to live again but differently. It took some time after love found me before I realized it was

here to rescue me. It took some time for love to show me it was already in my life - cheering me on, rooting for me, and praying God's best for me. Part of me didn't think I could get up from my self-imposed prison, but there was always something inside of me that kept me driven to live. God knew the real Crystal wanted to live and didn't answer my soul's cry to die. I've always been that way and many people can't believe it when I tell them about the things, I've experienced because of the resilience I display in the aftermath. Truth be told, when you have had experiences with the presence of God, you may have a lapse in memory and purpose but the God intelligence inside of you will awaken you and you'll know you have to get up and go live. Death and grief don't have to rob you of the joy for life; death is a *part of life*. Its existence helps us define life and our purpose in living. In the pages that follow is the story of my journey to this understanding.

i never dreamed you'd leave in summer

A Mother's Journey from Mourning to Morning

Chapter 1

What Happened?

Before I begin, I'd like to say I am now Mrs. Crystal Willingham. At the time this tragedy took place, I was married to Kevin Smith, the father of my children. I never have and never will dishonor him as the father of my children and particularly as Symara's father. Our divorce had nothing to do with the death of our daughter. Kevin and I both feel it necessary to stress this as a clear point of understanding. Statistically, and from the outside looking in, marriages struggle to survive - and couples often divorce, after the loss of a child. Suffice it to say that our marriage could be counted among those statistics. We don't feel the need to explain beyond that because that part of our journey is personal, and this is not a "tell all" book. Kevin was grieving too and deserves the honor and respect due to a father who has lost a child. We, Kevin and I, have had a conversation about this book and he acknowledges that this is my story.

I expected Kevin to be angry and upset with me when he arrived at the hospital that night in August, but he was genuinely concerned about me and the well-being of our other children. Kevin never once blamed me or made me feel less than competent as a mother for what happened, and I appreciate that more than I can express here. I can't tell his story for him, but I will always honor him as Symara's father. It

I Never Dreamed You'd Leave in Summer

is right to do so. With that being said, here is what happened.

On the morning of August 13, 2009, I got up early to prepare for our 12 to 15-hour road trip down Interstate 75, heading home for a visit. I am originally from Detroit, Michigan, where I was born and raised, and I hadn't been home since moving to Atlanta. Now let me get all the questions out of the way - or should I say - the question that is on most of my Christian family's church mind. Did you pray about this trip first? The answer is, "Yes, I prayed and more than once". So, I packed up clothes for five children and one adult for the long haul. At that time, my husband really didn't have enough days to take off to join us for the trip and decided to stay home. I did what most frugal mothers do on road trips: I packed sandwiches, juice boxes, and chips since our cash flow was quite low. So low, I wasn't sure about how much money we had for gas on the return trip. This trip home was more than just a visit. I had planned to connect with my pastors from Detroit and bring our goddaughter, Tiffany, back to Atlanta as well. I picked up the truck, borrowed from a friend by the name of Marcus, from the repair shop and paid the repairs and the insurance. I remember the insurance agent expressing his concern about us being on the road and I promised him I'd make it to Detroit well before the wee hours of the morning if he'd hurry up. He did stress to me that he had a bad feeling and felt I shouldn't be on the road alone. I again thanked him for his concern and went on about my day, scurrying around to make sure my affairs were in order so we could get on the road. In case you're wondering, yes, I do regret not listening to him. However, he wasn't someone that was in my space on a regular basis. To my recollection, no one called me and asked me not to go. They wished me the best and said the typical words "Call us when you get there". I have traveled by car alone with the whole family, and back again, on I-75 from Michigan to Georgia. No hiccups, no accidents,

I Never Dreamed You'd Leave in Summer

nothing out of the ordinary, and safely from point A to point B. I was always cautious, stopping for gas and making sure someone knew where and when I stopped. If I pulled off the highway for any reason, I'd always call home and make sure someone knew. That was, and still is, the way I travel. I felt I was safe enough with the travel habits I had to go on ahead as planned. I don't remember the exact time I left but I remember I left late enough to get to Detroit well into the night. I didn't especially like to drive at night with the kids, but I was anxious to leave Atlanta and get home safely.

Did I beat myself up about this? Yes, and as I write this book, I am talking with my other children to ask them how they felt and what they knew then, or remember, about this time. It's important to keep a dialogue open when you are dealing with tragic deaths because if there's any way the enemy can get in to destroy you and your relationships, he will. Satan, or anything that is connected to his kingdom of darkness, does not have the capabilities of compassion, consideration, or love for you in your state of mourning. He will use your mourning to steal the quality of life you have left. Having a tearful memory now and again is normal. Having ups and downs is normal. Operating in a state of resiliency where you might bounce back and keep moving forward is normal. Satan would have liked me to succumb to my grief but talking about death and pain helps me and my family continue to accept what has happened and persevere.

After getting the car packed, Kevin (I was at this time married to the father of my children) prayed with us and we loaded up and got into the car. But not before Symara had a moment and started to cry and say how much she'd rather stay at home with her daddy. If you're a parent, you already know how your children can sometimes be a little indecisive. I never made my children do anything they didn't want to do unless there was a very sensible reason not to allow them a

I Never Dreamed You'd Leave in Summer

choice. I considered leaving her home even though I wanted her to be with me. At the very last second, when we were about to unpack her stuff from the truck, she changed her mind again. "Are you sure, Symara?" Her reply was a definite yes and so we moved on and got on the road. From Atlanta to Tennessee stopped to get some gas and thought I should turn this into a bathroom break, seeing that I had children and their bathroom breaks are often unexpected. I was going to get some gas but when I looked at the needle, I felt I had enough to make it to Kentucky where the gas prices were always cheaper. I was really counting pennies on this trip and knew where to buy fuel. Maybe if I had decided to gas up on this stop, this day would have turned out differently? I can't say with any certainty.

    I stayed in the car with my infant son who was 5 months old at the time and sent the rest of the children off with wipes, sanitizer, and tissue to use the toilet. When the children were coming back to the car, Symara was crying at the top of her lungs and I jumped out of the car to see what the matter was. Chelcie, my oldest daughter, told me Symara smashed her finger in the door. I knelt to her level and asked her to show me and kissed her little boo-boo on her finger. Now, I'm that tough mom: you get 5 seconds to cry and then you have to shake it off and move on. I tried to teach my children that pain is a part of growing up. When you hurt, you get a little time to cry and then you have to go ahead. I didn't do that this time because I really felt as though she was trying to get a little more attention than normal.

So - I threw away some trash from the vehicle and buckled the children back in. I was focused on making sure they were comfortable and seated safely. I always did that and never took my good driving for granted. I made sure they had access to snacks and Chelcie had access to hair accessories. Symara's hair was a mess and I didn't have time to braid it up

I Never Dreamed You'd Leave in Summer

like I normally would on occasions like this. I taught Chelcie how to braid and she was pretty good at it, so the plan was for her to cornrow Symara's hair while we were on the road. I thought she'd have enough room to do it even though it was tight in the back seat. I placed the baby in his car seat. Symara and Sydnie (child number 4) in the middle seat belt, and Chelcie (my eldest) on the end directly behind me. Diamond, (my second oldest daughter) was quite tall for her age and met the requirements to be a front seat passenger. After I got all the kids situated, I hurried up and got back into the driver's seat because I wanted to get to my destination.

As we moved on down the road, Symara saw an 18-wheeler truck. I had taught them how to motion to the truck driver if they wanted them to blow the rig horn at them. Sure enough, she remembered that and got a truck driver to pull the horn just for her. What really got her attention was a few miles down the highway when we came upon the mountains. She totally lost it with excitement and was adamant about seeing mountains. So much so that she got out of her seatbelt and was hanging off the back of the seat to see them. We all fussed at her about getting into the seatbelt and, oh boy, she didn't like that. She cried so loud! Chelcie told her that if she didn't get back into the seatbelt mommy was going to get a ticket and go to jail. I always told them that wearing seatbelts was the law and they knew this. Sometime just before Symara got out of her seatbelt, I was engaging with Diamond, who's in the front seat, about cleaning the dashboard of all the dust that was on it. The AC wasn't working so we had to travel with all the windows down and dust kept flying everywhere. Between fussing with Symara about her seatbelt and cleaning the dashboard the moment that changed our lives happened.

    I was under the impression that the children had gotten safely back into their seatbelts as Chelcie had temporarily unbuckled herself to make sure her sisters were buckled in.

I Never Dreamed You'd Leave in Summer

Just after that, Symara quickly fell off to sleep. It's still a wonder to us how she went to sleep so fast after crying. Well, as I was showing Diamond how to clean the dash with my right hand, my left hand was on the wheel. I didn't see the little bend or curve in the road coming and was turning the wheel too sharply to the right to follow the lanes curving to the right. I almost swerved into the next lane and realized it with a start. I over-corrected my hand on the wheel and the truck toppled. I lost control of the truck!

We rolled over about 4 times and I had never been so scared in my entire life. I will never forget the screams of my children or the terror in Diamond's eyes as she repented to God for anything she had done wrong. She looked at me and called out to me, "Mommy, oh God, Mommy!" I looked at her straight in the eyes for a split second and told her, "Don't call me, call Jesus!" - and that is exactly what she did. We all did! I can never write or tell this part of the story without losing my breath or getting a knot in my whole body. I can't forget the look of horror on Diamond's face as long as I live. I will never forget the look of terror on Sydnie's face as long as live. I will NEVER forget Symara flying past me and I tried to catch her. I screamed out to JESUS because he was the only one that could help us at that moment. When we finally stopped rolling, I saw my baby girl hit the pavement. The truck had landed upside down. Half of my body was inside of the truck and the other half outside of the truck with my legs, and the truck, on top of Symara's legs. I looked upward and saw Symara's lifeless body on the ground and was panicked. I called out to the rest of my children but I didn't need to, I felt like they were ok. The one that I knew was *not* OK was right there, by some miracle of physics, in my arms. (As I always do, I literally lose air when I tell this part of the story. It reminds me that I'm human, this really happened, and she's really gone). I prayed frantically over her as bystanders rescued the rest of my children. I know my children were frightened, but I had to trust people to come to their aid since I was helpless to do anything, pinned as I was. Diamond was screaming at the people who were trying to get her out. She wanted them to help me first, but I knew it was going to be a long time before that would happen. I yelled out to Diamond to let them get her out and she went fighting. My son was unbuckled from his car seat and when I glanced at him before he was snatched out of it, he was smiling at me. Sydnie responded to my voice and she was pulled from the wreckage. Chelcie, however, got out of the car praying in her heavenly language. At the time, I didn't know she could pray like that; I thought what I heard was someone else who may have been an intercessor or something. I was only later informed that it was my daughter's voice I'd heard.

Just after we stopped rolling, I knew Symara was gone. I screamed at God, "Don't take my baby, please! Don't you take her!" There was a still small voice, one that I was familiar with, answer me back. "I've already taken her; you need to let her go!" Hanging upside down, I watched my children leave the wreckage. This time I wasn't screaming, I was tearfully pleading with God, "Please don't take my baby girl. Don't take her, take me instead. I lived long enough." That still, small voice said, "I've taken her, you have to let her go." I don't know how, seeing that I was upside down, but I hung my head down and cried. My reply to Him was, "Then I commend her soul to You." I wept and mourned her that moment. There wasn't anything anyone could tell me to convince me she was still here. I KNEW she was gone. Knowing in my heart she was gone wasn't enough. I needed a concrete confirmation of her death and nobody at the accident site was willing to give me that confirmation.

Several things were happening. While half of my body was pinned under and outside of the truck and the other half

I Never Dreamed You'd Leave in Summer

strapped in the seatbelt and hanging upside down, I had an epiphany. I'm in pain and I need the rescue workers to hurry up and get me and this truck off my baby girl. I started praying, "God I need you to help these workers come up with a plan to get this truck off me and Symara. Lord give them the wisdom and the expertise to get it done." Now I understand how unbelievable that sounds, but it was the only thing I knew to do. I was raised up in a Christian home and if my parents didn't do anything else, they prayed. My parents prayed, my grandparents prayed, the three churches I was actively involved in prayed, and they ALL taught me the power of prayer. Someone had run up to Symara and tried to pull her up from the ground, but I wouldn't let them. I screamed at them not to move her. First, I knew better - you don't move a victim without assessing the situation and second, she was pinned under me. In their zealousness to help, they didn't evaluate the safest way to intervene.

By the time the police got there, (keep in these events happened very fast), the officer in charge wanted to know why Symara had not been moved. The other police officer replied to him, "Ms. Smith told us not to move her." The officer in charge asked, "Since when do we listen to the victim on how to do our job?". The officer bent down into the truck to tell me that they are going to remove my daughter from the pavement. I told him, "No, you're not going to do that. My daughter's legs are pinned under my legs and my legs are pinned under this truck. You better get this truck off me so you can remove her without ripping her legs off." The officer finally looked and saw that I was right; he ran off to discuss with other responders the best way to get the truck off me. So, I prayed harder. I was in so much pain and I knew this was going to take a while. I remember thinking I needed to distract myself from the situation so I wouldn't lose my mind. The next thing I knew, I was singing every song I could think of that honored God. My first choice:

> "I love you Lord and I lift my voice.
>
> To worship you, oh my soul rejoice.
>
> Take joy my King in what you hear.
>
> Let it be a sweet, sweet, sound in your ear."

Ironically, it was the very first song Symara learned and sang all the way through by herself. I can attribute that to the mornings she spent with her father Bible reading and listening to praise and worship music. She would often come and sit with me if I was singing or worshipping at home. She was always around worshippers. At that difficult time, I did what I knew. A few times the officer bent down in the truck to talk to me and help me stay focused. I am grateful to him for that because he really tried his best. I remember telling him that he needed to pray to God and come up with a plan to get this truck off me. I told him that he hadn't prayed or talked to God since he was a child and that's what I needed him to do most importantly. The police officer later told my god-sister Stacy, who was at the hospital with me, that I told him the truth. I can't explain a lot of the things that happened on this day. All I know is God was present with me and I'm thankful for eyewitnesses who can attest to the wonder of God working throughout this life-changing occurrence.

Spending time singing praises to God, I can't tell you how fast time went. Afterward, I thought about my conversation with the officer and my worship session with God, guessing it took them about 20-30 minutes to get me out of the wreck. The police officer in charge told my god-sister it actually took them 2 hours to get me out from under that truck. I think the 20-30 minutes was what it took for them (with manpower) to get the truck lifted off me long enough to get Symara out from under me and the truck. I had no idea the elapsed time because it seemed to whiz right past me. We can chalk this up to science and say trauma, adrenaline, I passed out, or

I Never Dreamed You'd Leave in Summer

whatever notion you can come up with. I choose to believe God just gave me a supernatural grace and removed me from the situation until they could get me out.

When the rescuers got me out, I felt like I had just woken up as the evening air hit my face. I could no longer smell the odor of glass, metal, and gasoline fumes. I'll never forget that smell, it's lodged in my memory. I am a person of smell. To this day, I use and carry the original formula for Chapstick in my purse. The reason I carry it is because it reminds me of my innocence as a child and a time my father took me to see the Thanksgiving Day parade in downtown Detroit. Chapstick and hot chocolate are the smells I remember most from that wonderful day. This horrible day, though, I remember with the combined smell of broken glass, metal, and gasoline. Today, it doesn't send me in a downward spiral of emotions, but it sends me into a whirlwind of memories that help me remember how good God was to me during that event. Some of you may ask, "Why do such horrible things like this happen to good people?". I have an answer for that, but I'll get to it later.

As the night air hit my face, I was told I was being airlifted to the University of Tennessee Medical Center and was given morphine for pain. Initially, it was not expected that I would ever walk again because of the way my body was twisted in the car and the way my legs were mangled underneath the vehicle. Someone described my legs under the truck like the scene from "The Wizard of Oz" when the wicked witch of the east's house fell on her and her feet shriveled up under the house. That description alone sent chills all through my body again. I don't know who told me that, but I'll never forget it. Several times in the helicopter I reached out to an EMT to ask them about Symara. I told them it's okay for them to tell me she was dead, I just needed to know for sure. I was crying and pleading with them to tell me, but I think at some

I Never Dreamed You'd Leave in Summer

point they had given me another dose of morphine. Now that I think about it, they probably couldn't even hear me, but I didn't care, I wanted to be heard and have my question answered. I remember the tears rolling down my face and into my ears as I was on the stretcher face up. I just couldn't seem to wrap my brain around what happened. I thought about my other children and their father and how much I just changed their lives. I wanted to die in that helicopter to be quite honest. I just didn't want to live through watching the pain I caused my family. I knew I didn't have the heart to play the part of the hero mom I wasn't. I was in pain for them and felt as though I deserved whatever hand they dealt back to me.

    I don't remember much about my arrival at the hospital. What little I know is largely filled in by the words of one of my closest and dearest friends, Stacy. She is who I refer to as my god-sister in this book. Well, rightfully so. We practically grew up together. Her family and my family went to the same church and school. You'll understand why as you read what she recited to me over the phone. I transcribed them, verbatim and this is what she said:

"When I got to the hospital some of the nurses were in shock at who this woman was in the cardiac unit of the hospital. Of course, Crystal had not suffered a heart attack or anything, but it was the only unit that had a room available. The nurses shared with me a story of the head supervisor who happened to be stuck working extra hours that night because someone else had called in. This nurse was known to not take any mess from anyone and from what I was told, was going through a divorce. This particular nurse had stationed herself to meet Crystal at the door when she arrived at the hospital.

As Crystal was wheeled into the trauma center, she was clearly very alert and awake and some of the emergency room workers questioned the fact that maybe she had not received adequate pain medication and shouldn't even be awake. However; as they wheeled Crystal in, she grabbed the arm of that supervisor and told her "Everything is going to be ok; your marriage is going to be ok." Now, of course, Crystal could NOT have known about this woman's marriage because this was the FIRST time she had ever been there. That head nurse/supervisor went and found a quiet spot to cry. How could she have known that about this woman and her marriage situation? The nurses were also amazed at how alert Crystal was and that she was able to talk and communicate the way she was. She doesn't remember but hospital staff kept visiting her floor to see who this woman was that ministered to the head/supervisor about a life situation that she had no idea about.

The chaplain told me, "I am going to get the communion she asked for so when her husband arrives, we all can take it together." It was so peaceful. Jesus did what he said He was going to do; make it an awesome testimony.

I watched Crystal make decisions about organ donation, arrangements for Symara to be taken home and milk for little Kevin with the greatest of ease. Truly the Lord is a very present help in your time of need. In Crystal's weakness, He was strong. Once Kevin arrived, I prayed and asked the Lord to yet again give me the right words to say and He did. We all shared funny stories about me and Crystal's friendship, our church and growing up. It was peaceful. I felt my release to leave and go home. I was heavy-hearted upon entering the hospital but left with joy in my heart. I continued to ask the Lord to show up and. I knew I would never be the same and Crystal wouldn't either. I was honored that the Lord placed me in her life to be there at such a monumental time."

-Stacey L. Prater-White

I didn't remember this time in the hospital as Stacey told it; my memories seem to be somewhat hazy or disjointed in time. I do remember the woman standing over me as I was

I Never Dreamed You'd Leave in Summer

wheeled in. I also remember her leaving my side and crouching down in the corner to cry. I also remember the sensation of being wheeled and my clothes being cut off me, my wedding ring being cut off my finger, and several questions. "What year is it? Who is the President of the United States? What is your full name? What year were you born?". One question wasn't asked of me but asked of the EMT. "Why is she awake like this, was she given the recommended medication dosage?" The EMT replied to the doctor that I was given what was advised - and simply couldn't believe I was still awake. I remember thinking how tired I was and finally went to sleep. To this day, you can't make me go to sleep unless I am WAY beyond tired. I literally have to be "falling asleep standing up" for me to throw in the towel. Chalk it up to adrenaline if you'd like. I was just determined to not rest until I knew my other children were ok and that I had confirmation of what I already instinctively knew - my Symara was gone.

What happened next was that I was left in the hallway of the hospital for a long time. Long enough to beg someone for a phone so I can call ANYBODY from home. I was stopping everyone in the hallway who would listen and a few times I got somewhat of a cold shoulder. It could be the fact that some had pre-judged me and thought I'd been drinking. Whatever the case, I could only remember my former pastor's phone number, so I called him. Pastor Henry tried his absolute best to comfort me, but I knew the worst already. His voice cracked a few times on the phone and I'm sure to this day he doesn't know how much I understood. I deeply needed a familiar voice at the time. I'm grateful he was available and grateful for my church family helping me through this difficult time. I am indebted to them for their kindness, time, and generosity. Thank you, One Accord Ministries, Soul Harvest Ministries, Ellis & Ellis Funeral Home, the Smith family, and my family - the Davises.

I Never Dreamed You'd Leave in Summer

From that seemingly interminable time in the hallway I was transferred to a trauma care unit. What happened there is well-described by a nurse named Margaret, in an account she wrote on behalf of the nursing staff at UT Medical Center:

"This model of care story exemplifies several elements of the patient and family centered care embraced here at UT Medical Center. I believe the emotional support shared through several compassionate staff members played a role as important as any medical intervention involved for my patient Crystal."

Please allow me to tell you our story:

Looking back, it does seem to be a story of circumstance; a circumstance that Crystal was transferred to our unit where I, Margaret, had recently started working the night shift and, also, that our unit manager, Jada, was here during the night shift. This night, Jada was working to provide coverage for rounds so that nurses can attend necessary meetings.

As a result, Jada had spent time with Crystal in the emergency room. After midnight, I was notified that a trauma patient would soon be transferred to the unit and that I would be her nurse. Soon I received a verbal report detailing pertinent information about a young woman involved in a serious motor vehicle accident. This patient would be Crystal. I was terrified! I was not a trained trauma nurse! Immediately I informed my manager about the patient and that I was concerned about caring for the patient. She reassured me that I was capable of caring for Crystal. I began to pray that God would not only comfort and help my patient, whom I had never met, but that he would help me be the right nurse for her.

Within a few minutes, John, the ER team leader, called to speak with me about Crystal. He told me that he, the chaplain and the ER patient advocate, Jim, would be transferring my patient to the room and he requested that I be in her room waiting on her arrival. He stated that she was an out of state patient transported by Lifestar, who had been traveling alone with her five young children and that the children had been left at a local hospital in another county where the accident occurred. That is not all! He stated that after her arrival into the room we would inform her that her four-year-old daughter, Symara, had been killed in the accident and that her four surviving children were left at the hospital. Where would I draw the strength for this task?

As Crystal rolled into the room, our eyes met, and she immediately asked me about her baby and where were her other children? As we moved her over to the bed, she looked right at me and said, "I know you know. I know my baby is dead, but no one will tell me, please tell me about my baby." Then as gently as possible John, the ER team leader, confirmed that her four-year-old daughter had passed away at the scene of the accident. I will never forget the sound of her shrill scream, as she began to wail and cry uncontrollably. Right then

I realized that this young mother needed me. Everyone present tried to comfort her in the best way we knew; some by touch, some by reassuring her verbally and others by asking her information about her surviving children.

After the ER staff departed, Crystal just wanted me to hold her. I held her as close as I could. At her request, the chaplain & I prayed with her. That seemed to help her more than any medication. After we realized that Crystal had no friends or relatives in the Knoxville area, the chaplain tried to reach family members by phone. When she was unsuccessful, I called for my manager. As soon as Crystal saw my manager's face, she remembered meeting her in the ED. Another chaplain arrived with her personal computer and we all began using our cell phones to attempt to try to contact family. Crystal had been traveling from her home in Georgia to her father's, in Michigan. Her only contact in Tennessee was an old friend, Stacey, who lived in Nashville. After a lot of prayer and phone calls, we

I Never Dreamed You'd Leave in Summer

spoke with Stacey and she was able to give us phone numbers for Crystal's father. Stacey immediately rented a truck and headed to Knoxville. As soon as her father, Mr. Davis, heard the news of his daughter's crisis, he too started to Tennessee. Crystal's husband had been contacted by the hospital where the children were, and he was scheduled to arrive at the Knoxville bus station the next day. My manager and I spent the night trucking for Crystal and trying to comfort her. We contacted the other hospital for updates on her children, which seemed to help reassure her some. Crystal asked for a Bible but requested that my manager not leave her, so I left the room praying that I would find one quickly. Crystal asked my manager to begin to read scriptures, but Crystal would begin quoting the verses as my manager would begin to read the Bible.

As we begin to bathe her in attempt to remove all the glass slivers, Crystal began to tell us about the accident and when and how she knew her little girl, Symara, had died at the scene. We talked about how she believed her little baby was in heaven with her wonderful grandmother. As she requested, we sang, she sang, we prayed, and she prayed.

A few hours into the night, we realized that her husband would not have transportation to UTMC or to the other hospital to get their children after he arrived at the bus station. Our next task at hand was to find a way to get her husband to UTMC. We called the security department to pick up her husband at the bus station and after visiting his wife, he would transport him in a van provided by UTMC to pick up his children. A chaplain would ride along with them. That security guard and chaplain came to my patient's room and introduced themselves and reassured her they would be at the bus station to meet her husband. Our next dilemma, we needed two truck seats for the van. My manager suggested that I call the mother-baby unit for assistance and they arrived shortly and provided what we

I Never Dreamed You'd Leave in Summer

needed.

During this time, I seldom left Crystal's room. I knew I was needed in other rooms to give medications and other tasks. Then I heard a knock at the door and in walked Debbie RN, asking what she could do for me. She took my computer and completed the tasks that my other patients needed. I felt Debbie was an angel sent to me when I needed it most. What a team effort from all the hospital staff involved in this situation! Many went above and beyond their duties to help this young family, and I will never forget that.

Realizing that Crystal's friend and family could not arrive till later that day, I chose to stay at Crystal's bedside and soothe her fears and anxieties to the best of my abilities and to just be there to listen. I felt like I could not leave her alone!

As soon as her friend Stacey arrived, she climbed up in the bed with her and held her up close and the three of us prayed and gave thanks together. Crystal was no longer alone, so I went home. Later that afternoon I came back to the hospital to check on her and had the pleasure of meeting her family. What an honor to have been her nurse. To add to the story, it turned out a miracle happened when Crystal's father, Mr. Davis, rented his truck in Nashville from the same business that Stacey had rented from. His vehicle was upgraded (free of charge) to a van large enough to transport his daughter, grandchildren and all other family members. My manager and I continue to hear from Crystal and her family via email and Facebook. She and her family are doing well. She calls on our birthdays and we contact her on important dates in her family's life.

The physical and medical care given to our patients may not always be the most important care we provide. Being there for the emotional support, helping arrange services for things that will reduce stress for our patients and their families are sometimes the greatest gift we can give."

I Never Dreamed You'd Leave in Summer

When I arrived in my room, most of what Margaret said I did, I don't remember. I do recall bits and pieces but the most important part to me today was asking her to read God's word to me and discovering I could finish the scriptures she started. One thing I know was proven to me that day; God's word is life and written in your heart if you embrace it. I have a relationship with Him, His son, the words He inspired men to write, and that day His word became my breath. I remember John, and the sobering look on his face as he was giving me the news that Symara was gone. I remember that they dimmed the lights. Since they quickly discovered I was a religious woman, someone suggested putting the TV on TBN so I could have what is familiar to me in my space. I don't mean to sound insensitive, but now that I think about it, I felt like I was in a scene from Grey's Anatomy. I knew this was real, but I sure didn't want it to be. After I cried, I felt the essence of me leave my whole body and the only thing I knew to keep me alive was God, His words of comfort through the scriptures. I requested communion because I didn't want to give the enemy any room for him to take this and use it to destroy my family.

Everything I knew to do, to stay grounded and not lose my mind I did. I was shocked, devastated, and at times I could feel myself coming unglued. I just felt that I needed to be standing in strength for my family. There wasn't anything anyone could have said or done to deter me from feeling that way. My friend and sister Stacey came and did the unimaginable. She got into bed with me and held me as close as she could. I didn't realize how much glass was in my hair and skin until she brushed it out. Little slivers of glass kept coming up out of my skin. So much was going on as I was talking to Stacey: nurses were stopping by my room who were not assigned to me or my floor, and with all that activity, Stacey told me about a conversation she had with the police officer in charge at the accident site.

This is what Stacey said, "*This is where the Lord totally blew my mind. The officer gave me his account of what happened, and he said: "When we arrived at the scene, she was holding her daughter and praying. I felt a very faint pulse and she looked up at me and said: "She's gone, God already told me, now get my other children out of the truck." He said you then asked the officers to quote the 23rd Psalm while they were working at the scene. I was amazed that the Lord yet again was showing Himself strong in this situation. The officer was shocked that you didn't have any injuries; he saw you at the scene and was there when the helicopter came."*

Remember this, God is always in control. His word says that we can be sure that every detail in our lives is worked into something good (Romans 8:28, The Message Bible). I know you're thinking how this could possibly be for those that love

God? Why is something so ugly allowed to happen to them that love God as we do? The answer here is that the terrible things we experience don't come from the Lord, they come from the brokenness of the world. God is our shelter when we face the ugliness. It was His word that kept me alive when I couldn't breathe. The Holy Spirit, His comforter, was in that truck, in the helicopter, in the emergency room, in the x-rays, the MRIs, the CAT scans, in my room, and inside of me. Being a child of God doesn't exempt us from pain and human error. The cycle of life is referred to in James 4:14, "You don't know the first thing about tomorrow. You're nothing but a wisp of fog, catching a brief bit of sun before disappearing. Instead, make it a habit to say, 'If the Master wills it and we're still alive, we'll do this or that'" (The Message Bible). The wisp of fog named Symara came and left so very quickly and I was losing my ground. I just knew God wouldn't let me sink or drown. In the words of singer, Amanda Lindsey Cook, from her song

I Never Dreamed You'd Leave in Summer

"Comforter":

Where there are no words

    And even breathing hurts

    You're my comforter

    You won't abandon me

    You're with me in the deep

    And You won't let me sink

This will be my great redemption

    While I wept, he set my feet to dancing while I was relying on the Bible, the inspired words of God, songs of my Christian faith, and prayer to get me through the crisis.

    This was too much for me to bear alone and I didn't want to lean on anyone too much. I felt like everyone had their own pain to bear, without taking on mine, as well. My parents flew in from Detroit, Kevin's family members drove down from Detroit, and Stacey abruptly left her home, husband, and family to be at my side. I didn't want to be any more of a burden to them. I didn't know when to lean and when to stand. I winged it. Sometimes I let people tell me what to do, but I knew what I wanted to do for Symara's memory and for my family. No matter what was going on that day, despite the storm that just came into our lives - God was still in control.

The nurses and doctors couldn't seem to believe that I hadn't sustained any life-threatening injuries. However, for months afterward I had ringing in my ears and vertigo. I have a persistent limp, and some mobility loss in my left hand. It took months before I could feel my left foot completely. I was told later I did have some bleeding in my brain, but it seemed to correct itself. I was sent letters and referrals for restorative therapy just in case I experienced any longer-term aftereffects. I can't recall being examined by the doctor when I first arrived at the hospital - I was heavily medicated at the time. The doctor did see me, but the words the nurse spoke to me were something I couldn't live with. I wanted to know when I could

I Never Dreamed You'd Leave in Summer

leave and get to my other children. She told me when I could walk down the hall unassisted then I could leave. My legs were badly swollen and painful, but I didn't care. I wanted to see my children. The nurse followed me out of my room and she was holding my elbow. I looked at her and asked her once again, "Did you say I can't leave unless I can walk unassisted?" She confirmed it and so I kindly asked her to leave me alone, I can do this by myself. In the back of my mind, I thought I couldn't come undone right then but as soon as I got back to Atlanta, I'd yield to whatever this grief was like - no matter what it looked like. But NOT TODAY, today and the next many days to come belonged to my family.

    I was discharged hours later as I was walking down the corridor unassisted. They thought I wouldn't do it, but I was ready to get out of there and see my children; they didn't know that their sister had passed away and I wanted to be there with them when they heard it. Diamond later told me she thought she saw them place the sheet over Symara at the accident site and she settled it inside of her own self. Telling them cut me like a jagged-edged sword. Our son was only five months old and has no recollection of the incident whatsoever. My other girls, of course, remember it well and I was broken inside for them. Most of my family was supportive and comforting. Some, not so much; I had to remember Who I needed, and who needed me. Keeping my energy focused helped me bypass what was unimportant and keep my mouth shut about a lot of things. Our girls were heartbroken, and I could only trust God to help us help them. I believe my father prayed over us after they got the news and took us to eat dinner. To be honest, most of the trip from the hotel back to Detroit is a blur. I only remember clearly going to the site where the wrecked vehicle was to see if there were any clothes and belongings, we could salvage.

    Coming home and preparing to bury our daughter was

I Never Dreamed You'd Leave in Summer

something I dreaded, and I did my best to get through it. I smiled, greeted family, allowed my 'normal' self to be a part of the moments, but deep down in my gut I just didn't want to do it. I had originally stated I didn't want an open casket. Nobody could convince me to do that. I don't remember if I decided on my own or if someone talked me into it, but I finally gave in. I walked into the funeral parlor and sat in the back of the room. I didn't want to see her like this, and I felt paralyzed by the fact that the shell of my baby was lying there in a casket. I will never forget watching my parents, Kevin, and my cousin/sister Yulanda walk up to the casket and look at her. Although I was sitting in the back there was one distinctive physical attritubute of Symara I could see way in the back of the room. I always said she had the curliest eye lashes I had ever seen. Her eye lashes were so long and curly and that was what I spotted first from way in the back of the room. That drew me and I left my seat towards the casket. I couldn't believe it was her, but I also knew it was her. There she was, right in front of me and gone at the same time. The assistant funeral director began to talk about the presence of God that came into the room when he tended ot her. He told us how he had to improvise and create sleeves for her because the dress I brought for her didn't cover the bruises on her arms. The woman that did her hair began to tell me how she cared for her as if this was her own child. I couldn't' thank them enough for the care and delicacy in which Ellis funeral home took care of our needs.

    The Homegoing Service was beautiful and for a long time afterward, people would continue to tell us they'd never seen a service quite like it. I agree - her celebration of life was a beautiful occasion. I am grateful for the people who helped us find the money to have her funeral. We were not able to bury her that day or be there when she was buried. The funeral home would not release her body until we gave them the

I Never Dreamed You'd Leave in Summer

money for her service. We couldn't stay in Detroit until her life insurance policy was ready – it would take longer to get the policy settled than we realized. To this day, there's a hole in my heart about that; more on this topic later. I'm choosing not to go into details of her homegoing celebration to honor that memory for my family. After we said our goodbyes and boarded the bus back to Atlanta, it just seemed like a world of pain was waiting for me there. I had left with five children and was returning home with four. My questions to God were how and why? Here is the reason I am writing this book. The second leg of this journey started when we put the key in the door at 876 White Street and tried to live again.

God's word is life and written in your heart if you embrace it.

Chapter 2
Now What?

Putting my key in the door and trying to find a new normal was difficult for me - and remained difficult for a long time. What I felt could be best described as claustrophobic and desperate to find whatever that new normal was. I remember going to her bedroom and sitting on the bed to smell her clothes.

I went into the bedroom, shut the door, and wept. I had finally let go. I did, with all the strength I could muster, made it my business not to come unglued for the sake of the children. I felt that I was doing the right thing only to find out later, I may have done an injustice by not showing them how to release their tears properly. I don't remember much of this part of my life. Somethings I remember but not in sequential order or some parts may be unclear or missing. The one thing I am confidently sure about is that I missed her so much. Eventually I gathered all her clothes and placed them in a plastic bag. My goal was to have someone sew a quilt for me and I would put it in a glass frame and hang it on the wall. I had actually planned to raise money and do this for other moms as well.

It was hard to find the new normal at first. Some things I did routinely I just couldn't get away from. One example of something that was difficult but I had to learn to do concerned

I Never Dreamed You'd Leave in Summer

our shopping routine. At the time, my family was struggling financially and I was able to apply for food stamp assistance. It was my routine that at the first of the month, I let the kids pick out their favorite cereal. No matter how much it cost, I told them they could get it - just the way they like it. No generic versions of their favorite cereal would be allowed! It might sound crazy, but it was tough buying three boxes of cereal instead of four for the first time.

I always shopped for my kids in pairs. In my mind, it was always Chelcie & Diamond, Sydnie & Symara. Chelcie and Diamond grew up a year and two weeks apart. Sydnie and Symara were a year and 2 months apart. I would buy in twos for my girls because they were perfectly coupled up. Going to the store to buy Sydnie a shirt or pair of shoes and then automatically walking the aisle to find the same shoe in a smaller size had been usual for me. My new normal was just taking the time to acknowledge Symara's absence; I may have shed a tear and tried to make Sydnie feel as special as I could.

I mentioned earlier how the loss of a loved one affects us differently and is related to their role in our life. I've never lost a spouse or parent so I can't speak to those losses, but I can relate to the loss of a child. A miscarriage or stillborn child is still the loss of a child but experienced differently than the loss of a child that you have had the opportunity to raise. I've experienced a miscarriage and it affected me deeply; I mourned that baby leaving my body under hostile circumstances. I was under stress and I let something get to me and worry me so much, my unborn baby couldn't live there. I was preparing to have another baby on Monday and mourned the loss of that same baby on Thursday. Therefore, finding a new normal depends on what the old normal was for you. In the case of my miscarriage, I made the new normal adjustment as quickly as possible. I wanted to get on with my life.

I Never Dreamed You'd Leave in Summer

After Symara passed, I had to get used to her absence on earth and I knew this. I told myself this new normal was a place I wanted to reach. I had this conversation with myself many times, but that's where I stopped. I told myself I wanted life to go on in a new way, but at the same time, I refused it. I didn't want to accept it as a gift because I was still feeling weighed-down, hurt, and condemned for not protecting her. In other words, I didn't think I deserved to move in to a new normal; I was instead at a standstill, punishing myself for Symara's death.

For a long time, I was upset with God and I told Him about it. I did a lot of talking to God, but I wasn't doing much listening. I felt perturbed because other people were telling me about the wonderful encouragement they got from me discussing my journey through losing my daughter, yet I felt no peace. As I prayed one day, voicing my frustration to God, He stopped me dead in my tracks. This day I stopped talking and listened. Boy, did God have something to say. I can't say if this was a vision or what, but I was immediately taken to the cross. I saw the thief that hung with Jesus, asking Him to remember him when He enters the Kingdom. Here is Jesus being taunted by one thief, but petitioned by another, while he was bleeding out on the cross. I was reminded that every pain that I could ever experience physically, emotionally, and spiritually, Jesus bore on the cross for me, in lieu of me, He did it all for me. The message was:

"If I in massive suffering and pain could minister to one thief, you can minister about this part of your journey to those I choose for it to reach. You've already allowed me to do this through you - you are just feeling down today. Think about the police officer you ministered to while you hung upside down in that truck. You ministered to the hospital administrator who was there when you were wheeled into the hospital. When the administrator at the social security office was heartless and

mean to you, you ministered correction to her. If you allow Me to heal you and use this for My glory, the testimony of My love for you will be seen."

There were more times than not that God showed me how powerfully He was moving in my life and I missed it. Let me tell you, there were times when God did some things during this part of my life that were so amazing to me. I had to learn to be grateful amid something I couldn't truly understand. The God of the universe, the Creator of heaven and earth, was, is and will continue to be God. My pain doesn't change who He is, it changed how much more I saw who He is to me.

Some people told me that they had dreams about Symara and how much those dreams blessed them. As for me, I had a few nightmares, sleepless nights, and memories of rolling around in the truck watching my baby girl fly past me without me being able to grab her and hold onto her. Why couldn't I think fast enough to catch her? Better yet, why weren't they all strapped in? So many questions and not enough answers. I kept asking God "why would this happen to me? I serve you, I love you, and I would never walk away from you, so God, explain this one to me." I've been through quite a bit of trouble in my life as it was, but this took the cake. Did I think I would ever recover? No, and for a while I made sure that I didn't accept recovery. I thought I was healing but, trust me, this process was something else – something beyond what I was prepared for. I wanted to punish myself for what happened, and I even let a few outsiders convince me that it was okay to just be the below-par, mediocre person I deserved to be. Oh, yes - condemnation was killing me softly and slowly because I never let on that it was ripping me to shreds. I was self-sabotaging my career, my ministry, and my life with negative thoughts. No matter what anyone said to me, I didn't and couldn't accept that God still had a plan for my life. Yes, I

I Never Dreamed You'd Leave in Summer

was a functioning woman in ministry, in deep pain. But somehow, I just kept right on going.

It's amazing to me how the grace of God works for us while he works in us. God was still working through me, using me, allowing others to see Him in me. In the middle of all of this, I was still growing, maturing, and making some mistakes as we all do in life. The preaching and speaking engagements continued, the first book was published, and there were a few other things that I got to participate in career-wise that filled my time. But that void I felt so often? I didn't allow God to fill it for quite a while because I felt as though I deserved the pain that void contained. I did finally realize I could never punish myself for my mistakes, Jesus took that at the cross for me. The only thing left for me to do was accept that truth and leave my pain at his feet. For a long time, though, I'd leave it and then go pick it right back up.

I can remember being sore in my soul and had a talk with

God. I wanted Him to give me answers - and I wasn't hearing them. I kept going back to God in prayer, worship, and fellowship but I realized one thing. Every time I went to Him with my questions, His presence was better than any answer I would have gotten. His presence was soothing, healing, and He was so patient with me. In the back of my mind, I knew His answer wouldn't satisfy me enough to bring me peace. I was habitually talking myself out of that peace. Let me be clear about the understanding I had of what death was for Symara: I knew where her place was, what that meant for her life in eternity, and how that was a blessing to my soul. My baby was with her Father in heaven and among the cloud of witnesses. The outcome of my human error that fateful day was that my baby girl was with her Father in heaven. Although she was living in a place I was longing to be at the end of my days, it was my fault she was there. It all seemed pretty straightforward. Be that as it may, I still had questions I wanted

God to answer. I don't remember them specifically, but if I know me, I wanted him to tell me if my daughter was aware of me. Did she know how much I loved her, and did she know her mommy was so sorry for not protecting her? God, can you tell her I'm sorry?

My nights were hard, but I knew how to fight through them. I would play a lot of worship music while I slept. My god-daughter would make sure my favorite worship songs played for me throughout the night. Tiffany couldn't have been more sensitive to me about that. Now, as a child who had nightmares repeatedly, I learned at a young age how to bring Jesus into your night season so you can fight "the boogie man". Once I figured out how to do that, the nightmares ceased. Ever since then, I found ways to make sure I kept my atmosphere charged with His presence when I'm sleeping. God always prepares us for the things that happen in life, good or bad. The Bible tells us that all things work together for our good. When you are yielded to His divine purpose, ALL things work for you even though some things seem to be the worst things that could happen to you. Having nightmares as a young child taught me how to fight when the enemy would try to steal my sleep from me. I have shared this learning with my family so that they, too, know how to fight the enemy in sleep.

One night I fell asleep and drifted into a dream. I was sitting in a chair in the middle of a room and my children were running circles around me in a playful manner. As they were running and playing in a circle, I noticed Symara was also in the circle running. I let her run around a few times because I didn't really believe it was her. The last and final time she appeared, I called out to her. "Symara, come here. What are you doing here? You're not supposed to be here." She stopped running and jumped into my lap and said, "I just came to tell you that I love you." She kissed me on my face

I Never Dreamed You'd Leave in Summer

and I said, "Thank you Symara, thank you so much." I told her she could go now, and she went back into the circle with the rest of my children running circles around me. However, when it was her turn to appear again, she was gone, and I woke up. No, I don't believe that she literally came to me. I believe God gave me a dream to let me know that she loved her mother. I realize from this experience how much God cares for us even in our trauma and pain. He cared enough to give me a dream about her and let me experience a part of her that was real. The songwriter Civilla D. Martin wrote, "His eye is on the sparrow, I know he watches me." I had to learn to trust God's plan for recovery from this tragic moment for me.

I knew the enemy would use my daughters' death against me and my family somehow. Outside of the normal emotional reactions to her absence, I knew he would try to play me like an out of tune piano. Sometimes I allowed it not realizing that that was what I was doing. I knew the enemy was going to try to interrupt my new normal somehow, but I wasn't prepared for how he did it. The ways he could do it was through me, through other people, and other circumstances that had absolutely nothing to do with my daughter's death. Trauma has a way of intertwining its way into various aspects of our life. If we don't know or recognize this, it'll start to run your life. You'll miss the new normal God is creating for you if you are ignorant of the tools the enemy can use against you. God is fully aware of the emotional fulfillment people bring into our lives. He's also aware of the void that appears when that person leaves this earth. He wants us to let Him be in that void and be the emotional fulfillment we need until we are healed. If we let him, God will close that void and give us emotional freedom to continue. He gives us new relationships to fill that time and space if we allow Him to do it. I passed up a few real relationships because I didn't understand this initially.

I Never Dreamed You'd Leave in Summer

God wasn't allowing new needy relationships, but the ones that were fulfilling and timely. I accepted new relationships with people who fit the rhythm of my life. I never intentionally or with deliberate harm excluded anyone. I was moving into a new place with Christ Jesus, and in doing so I found my own peace - and I found a new normal. My new normal wasn't all about how to continue without Symara, it was about how to continue with God as the leader in my changed circumstances. My new normal became talking to someone, the right someone, about my feelings and how these feelings affect my daily interaction with my children. If I wanted to talk about Symara, I did. But only with people who wanted to listen and not people who just tolerated me because I was a grieving mother. I wasn't grieving anymore, I just wanted to talk about my child and share the few wonderful stories I have about her. My children were remarkable in sharing stories. We have some memorable stories about Symara's shenanigans because she was a four-year-old jokester if we ever knew one! She was witty, funny, precocious at times, and very intuitive in the last few months she was here. She had encounters with God that leave us speechless to this very day. Whenever I am asked to come speak about the loss of a child, I tell these stories and people are just as amazed as we were the day they happened. My new normal wasn't without Symara, but my new normal was with God.

Today, I am still an advocate for wearing seatbelts and I speak out about distracted driving. I have always supported seatbelt laws and I never pulled out of the driveway or parking spot without making sure my children were strapped in. The things I did at the last gas-station stop I made before the accident will always bring me peace of mind - knowing I did my job as a mom. I made sure my children were in those seatbelts. Sydnie and Symara occupied the middle seatbelt and had elbow room to stretch. Chelcie was in the seatbelt

I Never Dreamed You'd Leave in Summer

behind the driver's seat and even though she's the oldest, if you've ever seen Chelcie, you know she is very small and petite. She wore a size "0" in pants up until the day she became a mommy herself. Diamond, my second oldest would not have been able to sit in the back with two little people. She was and still is tall and used to be mistaken as the eldest. She was wearing her seatbelt as well. My 5-month-old son, Kevin Jr., was secured in his car seat - without a doubt. For so many years I blamed myself for Symara's death. Everything that happened in the truck happened in less than a minute and the series of unfortunate events didn't happen because I was a negligent mom. It was an accident, human error, and something I live with every single day. My new normal is living with a tragedy I can't change and letting my story be told to bring healing to other parents who are hurting.

Death and grief don't have to rob you of the joy for life; death is a *part of life.*

Chapter 3
Mourning & Grieving

Merriam-Websters a child defines mourning as an outward sign of grief. Mourning is what people do to recognize and mark the passing of a loved one. It is comprised of the customs, ceremonies, rituals, activities we do that formalize the beginning of the grieving process (wearing black, sitting Shiva, singing at a wake, holding funeral ceremonies, home going celebrations, etc.). Mourning customs vary from culture to culture, social group to social group and there is usually a mourning period - a specific beginning and end. Grief is defined as distress as a result of or caused by loss. Grief is the pain you feel when someone dies. It's a manifestation that comes out of your soul and is displayed many ways. Grieving is the process we go through when we have lost someone or something significant and refers to the internal emotions we feel and stages we may need to pass through in order to assimilate the loss into our experience, creating a "new normal" way of living.

    When my father heard about the accident, I was told he began to throw things around the room. My father said he didn't remember doing that and I can understand how. His immediate reaction to the bad news was an outward expression of the pain he felt. This contrasts with his calm and concerned demeanor when he arrived at the hospital. I have seen people withdraw and become over-taken with grief at a

I Never Dreamed You'd Leave in Summer

loss. Some lose their purpose or sense of reality because they are living in the past where that person existed. For some people grief becomes an affliction or much like a sickness: our physical body will react to grief if you give it that kind of control.

As much trauma this incident caused me, I didn't want to remain grieving because of my remaining children. They still needed a mother and I didn't want anyone else to have to step up and take on my role. In my mind, at the time, I caused my children pain, discomfort, and emotional disruption and I needed to stay focused enough on the routines of life so that I could make sure they kept going. I wasn't perfect but I did my best under the circumstances. I took what grief was giving me and turned it into faith for my children. If I was going to remain here, if God saw fit for me to stay on earth, then it was my conviction I was here to make sure they got a mother's love and move forward in their own lives.

Grief doesn't put a timestamp on how long you mourn someone's death. Grief, however, can keep you in a prison and disconnected from life around you: the result will be that you'll only be focused on the death, the void, and the emptiness you feel because of that person's absence. Wherever your focus is, that's where you will live. As long as you're living and breathing your focus should be living your life to the fullest with purpose, drive, and determination, giving God His place in the void that you feel. God is all-knowing, all-seeing, and everywhere - omnipresent and omniscient. He foreknew of the joy, triumphs, victories, and pain you'd endure in your life. As for the pain, God has always made a way to bear up under its pressure. He set it up before you were born. Hebrews 12:2 entreats us to look to Jesus who is the beginning and finisher of our faith. Jesus, who endured the cross for us and our suffering. His sacrifice is the example of perfect faith, perfect surrender in the face of the unbearable.

I Never Dreamed You'd Leave in Summer

When I was inside of the vehicle screaming at God not to take my daughter away from me, I thought about the consequences of God granting my request.

If God didn't miraculously heal her right then what would her life be like? I'm going to be very honest with you: I didn't want Symara to die because that would mean I failed all my children. I didn't want to bear the shame of my failure to protect her. I knew without confirmation that my other children were ok. They walked away with a few cuts and bruises and that was a miracle. I could never pick one child and say, "Take that one instead", but I did say, "Take me instead". Why wouldn't God just heal her right then? I can't answer that - and I stopped looking for the answer. I stopped searching because I recalled some occurrences that happened a few months leading up to the day she passed.

It was spring of 2009 and we didn't have a car. I told my family "Get up and get dressed - we are going for a walk". Our son was just a little bitty baby but I felt like it was time for him to breathe the spring air. I wanted to be out in Creation enjoying the smells, the sounds, and the greenery that spring brings. So, we walked to the neighborhood library taking it all in. Wouldn't you know it, the library was right next to Willie Watkins Funeral Home and yes, you guessed it, there was a funeral going on right then. Whoever had passed away was going to be taken to the cemetery in a horse drawn buggy. Because of her curious nature, Symara was intrigued by the whole event but I was really hoping we could pass by without her noticing it. Well, out popped the questions, starting with "Mommy, what's that horse doing over there on the buggy?". I had to explain to this inquisitive little person the workings of a funeral. The hardest part was explaining what a casket was and what, or who, was in it. I don't remember everything I said to her but I do remember on the way back we took another route because I really don't like talking about death. I had

I Never Dreamed You'd Leave in Summer

outrageously vivid nightmares about caskets, funerals, and death when I was a child and I just didn't want to open that door for the kids, so I kept the conversation as light as possible. As I grew up and gained an understanding of the practices and rituals our culture has for mourning the death of a loved one, the nightmares ended and I was able to embrace the reality of someone passing away. My goal that day was to make sure that Symara understood that. I knew my other children were listening so I used the unexpected occasion to turn it into a lesson for all. I reminded my children that if we confess Jesus Christ here on earth, our death on earth is the next phase of life for us. To my recollection, my parents didn't really explain death to me at the age of four. I think most of us never even think of explaining death to a four-year-old. However, my husband and I were the kind of parents that found ways to answer her so she could understand and accept the answers given to her at her level. Symara asked so many questions that day that her father and I looked at each other, silently sharing the thought that it was strange how mature her questions were. I just chalked it up to Symara being the inquisitive one in the bunch and resolved to stay ready to answer whatever questions she had.

    Fast forward to June of 2009. I was in my room, on my bed, tapping away at my computer, trying to write a play or perhaps getting ready to cast for a play. My son was asleep next to me. Symara came into the bedroom and decided to make my floor her playground for the day. She had gathered a collection of my lotions, perfumes, and "lady stuff" off my dresser and started role-playing with them. Her father's deodorant was the "man", my perfume was the "lady" and the little bottles of lotion were the kids. Off she went in her world of imagination. I love to hear children play, especially role-playing because I get a kick out of what they create in that world. As she played and I typed, Symara said, "Mama, can I

I Never Dreamed You'd Leave in Summer

ask you a question?" I am telling you as sure as my name is Crystal, I stopped what I was doing and all my antennaes went up. Symara never set up her questions, she always just came right out and asked them. I stopped typing and looked her straight in the eye, "Yes you can ask me a question." The next thing that came out of her mouth almost sucked the oxygen out of the room. "What's going to happen to me when I die?" Yup, she asked. At first, I was floored. I felt like the room was suddenly airless and the sound barrier was broken. Then I thought, maybe we need to pray because her questions have been pretty deep lately. Panic filled my mind for a few seconds until I heard a still, small voice saying, "Answer her question." I told her, "Symara when you die you'll go be with Jesus." She repeated, "Ok Mama, when I die, I'm going to see Jesus?" I answered her confidently, "Yes, when you die, you'll go be with Jesus." Before you ask, yes, she knew who Jesus is. The next question alarmed me even more. "When you die, are YOU going to see Jesus too?" I told her, "Well Symara, that's the plan. I want to be with Jesus when I die too. That will be a long time from now - because mommy will die before you will." She looked at me strangely as if I was talking a foreign language. I asked her, did she repent of her sins? She said, "Yeah Mommy, I did a long time ago already," or something to that effect. I began to explain again that it would be a LONG time before she would have to deal with that. She got up off the floor of my bedroom where she was playing and left the room with a simple, "Ok Mommy." Of course, this wasn't the kind of conversation I wanted to have with my four-year-old girl but, as usual, I answered Symara's questions as they came.

    Symara was also very witty and liked to play jokes on you, so you never knew what would happen or come out of her mouth. It was characteristic of her to be light-hearted and fun loving. Looking back, the seriousness of her questions and a change in her nighttime behavior was strange. The last few

I Never Dreamed You'd Leave in Summer

months she was here, she would sneak into our bedroom and climb into bed with us; we never knew she'd gotten in it until she kicked us. A few times I got up in the middle of the night to use the bathroom and I tripped over her because she was asleep on the floor. Some way, somehow, I think she was trying to tell me something. Maybe she knew she was leaving.

I'm telling you this story for no other reason than this: God always gives us a heads-up on what lies ahead. Sometimes we don't catch it at the time He shows us. Many times, we don't know we've gotten that heads-up until after something has happened. Living a life openly and transparently with God will show us what's ahead and we will know it's from Him. You don't have to be a Christian to understand that. Just a little side note; if we think that God only speaks to Christians, we are sadly mistaken. God is God and He can speak to whomever He chooses. You don't have to be a Christian for him to care and display his love for you.

I Peter 5:9 explains that the enemy is prowling about, roaring like a lion looking for someone - anyone - to devour. As Christians, we are taught to resist the devil but we are not exempt from the same kind of sufferings as our brothers and sisters not of the faith experience. In other words, the world will suffer pain, sicknesses, diseases, and death. Christians do not get a pass on any of the ills of life, however, the one who knows and believes in the God of Abraham, Isaac, and Jacob will endure it. The enemy doesn't care that you've lost the love of your life, your child, best friend, pastor, mentor, etc. His only job is to use any pain he can to kill your love of life. His job will always be to suck the life out of you by any means necessary. Don't let him use the wonderful life you have, or the life of the one you loved and lost, against you. Defeat him by living forward and sharing the memory of that loved one with the people in your life who love you. Defeat the prison of grief by intentionally finding the joy of living with the people in your

I Never Dreamed You'd Leave in Summer

life who are still here. Notice I keep using words like living and life? It's important to know and realize every single day, death is a part of life, not the end of life. As long as you remain here, you are charged to live forward.

Crystal P. Willingham

Defeat him by living forward and sharing the memory of that loved one with the people in your life who love you.

Chapter 4
TRIGGERS & TRAUMA

Before Symara's death, I wasn't very knowledgeable about trauma. As a matter of fact, that wasn't a word used frequently in the black community, the black family, nor the black church family. As a child, when somebody died, you cried about it. There was a sequence to be followed: you had the wake on Friday, the funeral on Saturday, with lunch at the church after the burial, you laughed and reminisced with fellow mourners, and then you went home. Church on Sunday, packing up the deceased person's belongings on Monday, and off to work on Tuesday. We used words like mourning and when we showed up to mourn someone's death, that's what we did. We cried and cried hard. We sang songs that made us feel the reality of that person's death. If you've never been to a black church family funeral, it's quite an emotional experience. We've moved on from calling it a 'funeral' to calling it a homegoing celebration. We now celebrate the life of our dearly departed instead of mourning their death. We've changed the language of mourning but we haven't changed the universal experience of pain and loss. Nor do we prepare ourselves for facing the resurfacing of our pain when triggered.

We don't always recognize our triggers, those events or circumstances that recall to us our traumatic experiences.

I Never Dreamed You'd Leave in Summer

Triggers that cause our souls pain may sometimes be labelled demons. However, we discover or label them, we need to be aware of them so that we might turn them to a life-giving advantage.

I now understand certain life situations may trigger memories of the pain I endured. October 26th, 2004 was Symara's birthdate. When the death certificate was faxed to us in Detroit, her time of death was stamped 10:26pm. When I saw the time '10:26' it acted like a trigger to my soul and I reacted in pain. Since then, I have found ways to make sure that 10:26 didn't send me into a full-on crash. While I had to learn to give in when needed so God could heal me, I also learned not to let the pain of grieving rob me of the quality of life or the joy of living in best moments of your life.

There were times when I would find myself grieving after months of being ok and going about my life only to discover it was the month of August or the last week in

October. To cope with these triggers, I began to intentionally create projects to keep me busy during those tough times, things that would require me to give back. For example, I would do a radio show targeted towards mothers and women. I found myself in gratitude of giving instead of pitying myself for the pain both I and my family felt. There was no better way of escape but for me to focus on living. I made a conscious decision to not allow Symara's memory to be wasted or tainted. She told me some very powerful things before she left and I hold on to those things to this day. Whenever I feel like life is suffocating me, I run to God first, because I know in my mind the enemy is coming for me. Satan will use my daughter's death to torment me. The Bible says in John 10:10, "The thief comes only to kill, steal, and destroy. There is no prerequisite for that other than the enmity God placed between Satan and the seed of humanity. He is incapable of compassion, leniency, or grace so don't expect it. Expect him

I Never Dreamed You'd Leave in Summer

to take every circumstance and situation you may find yourself in, including death, to rob you of the quality of life Jesus died to give you. The latter part of John 10:10 says, "Jesus came that they might have life and that more abundantly". Jesus paid the price for whatever the enemy of humanity tries to do to you. If the enemy can keep you focused on the pain and not being alive and living well, then he's winning the war against us. Jesus became our doorway to living our lives in full. We are like sheep and He is our pasture where we graze and receive anything we need. He's the Good Shepherd over us and whatever ails the sheep, He tends to it.

Once I realized Satan had a strategy to destroy me, I began to see my testimony of my recovery from a painful situation as a weapon to use against evil and I knew the devil couldn't defeat me any longer. Every time I spoke of my journey through loss to God's healing peace, his power became less and less evident and the words of the Gospel of Peace sprung up from the well inside of me. I could then recall the words that Symara spoke to me three days before she passed away. God used her to speak to me and I'll never forget what she said to me. It was a Sunday morning and I was fussing with God, aggravated about our financial situation. I was a faithful giver to the ministry I was assigned to, and we had help in the house with our bills, but you know how it is: towards the end of the month you end up with more month than you had money. I was frustrated and called my sister in the faith, G, on the phone. I told her our funds were already depleted, yet we had so much we wanted to do at home and with the people at our ministry. G suggested that we pray together about it and, I won't lie to you, I didn't feel much like praying that day. I felt too agitated in my soul to talk to God that day but she pushed me to pray anyway. After a few minutes of praying together we hung up the phone. I walked into the living room and turned on my "soaking" music, to charge my ecosystem with

I Never Dreamed You'd Leave in Summer

worship and God's presence. Then I called for the rest of the family to come together and pray with me as well. We all ended up gathering in the living room listening to the music and consulting with God together.

There was an undeniable and powerful presence of God in that room that day. I asked my family if they felt it too, and for each of them to tell me what they felt in the room. Each of my children, except for Kevin Jr, who was a little tiny baby, and Symara were able to answer me. I asked each of them if they felt anything. Each one of them, in their own way, told me they saw angels in the room. What they told me they saw and felt, flesh and blood did not reveal to them. They had tapped into the Spirit and saw what I felt. I believe it was Diamond who described a breeze that came past her. I tried to blame it on the air conditioning unit, but once I saw where she was seated, not in the path of the airflow, there was no way I could dismiss her words. I asked Symara's father Kevin, then

Chelcie, Diamond, and Sydnie. I didn't ask Symara because the occasion was so sobering and I knew her well enough to know that she could take a serious moment and flip it upside-down. She had a way of taking a room to from calm to levels of frenzy and laughter, even when we were trying to be serious.

But she let me know that I wasn't going to get away with skipping her on this one. "You didn't ask me Mama!" were her exact words and I was surprised she even noticed. She was sitting next to me on the couch and I turned to her and asked, "Ok Symara, what do you see?" She looked straight ahead at the front door and told us that she saw a "portal". I was alarmed but I didn't hesitate to get more answers from her. I said to her, "Symara, do you see God in there?" She answered me back, "No, but I know He's in there." For those who don't know me, I don't care how tense a situation is, I'm going to push the envelope and ask questions even if the answer is terrifying. So, the next question I asked her was, "Symara, what

I Never Dreamed You'd Leave in Summer

do you see in there?" She said, "Mommy, I see a treasure box with white diamonds, blue diamonds, red diamonds, and some of the other colors I don't know". Symara knew her colors, so I believe if she saw colors she couldn't name, then she must have had eyesight into a dimension that wasn't the norm for her. I asked her the next question: "Symara, is God telling you to say something to me?"

 "Yeah, give me a minute."

At this point all eyes were on her and we were anxious to see and hear what came out of her mouth. Her father, who was praying to himself, stopped his own prayer vigil to look at Symara in wonderment. So, we waited, and waited, and then she announced she was ready to speak.

She said, "Mommy, God says he has treasures for you".

I asked her, "Do you know what they are?"

She replied, "Yes, but I can't tell you."

She slid off the couch and left the room to go play. I was stuck in my position on the couch and couldn't believe what I'd just heard. Then again, I could believe it because it was Symara - and I knew and had experienced God using children, especially mine. I wasn't sure what to do with that information, as you see; despite what happened, maybe because of it, I was not going to forget that Sunday.

As you might know, you can't really detach yourself from the emotion of a loss. It's impossible, because you're human. We try, though, very often because that emotion is painful. Without thinking, we react to things that trigger our memories and emotions related to the death of a loved one. When you experience the death of a child your triggers may be set off in the activities you perform as a parent. For instance, like the shopping experience I related earlier, I was in the clothing store about to purchase some clothes for the kids. I have 4 girls and I tend to think of them in sets. Chelcie and Diamond are my first set who are only one year and two weeks

I Never Dreamed You'd Leave in Summer

apart. Then there was Sydnie and Symara who were a year and 8 months apart. Typically, if I bought Chelcie a shirt then I'd get one for Diamond. The older they got the less frequently I bought them identical outfits; their individual personalities began to flourish so I had to look for different styles of clothing for each girl. One day I was picking up some clothes on sale for Sydnie from Target. It was almost fall and Target was selling off their summer inventory. I would normally stock up by buying a size up; then I would have clothes for them for next summer. On this day, I was shopping, picking up clothes for Sydnie and immediately shifted to the smaller sized for Symara. I stopped myself, but not before that knot in my throat caught me and tears blinded my sight. I felt her absence and it overwhelmed me. I would normally try to ignore what I was feeling, but this time I just stood there and acknowledged my emotions. I let my tears happen, took in a deep breath, put the shirt back, and called for Sydnie to come stand with me while I continued to shop.

Before I got to this moment, my usual response was to disconnect from my feelings because I felt as though I didn't deserve to feel anything. I blamed myself for Symara's death and this numbing of emotion was how I was managing to cope. It wasn't until I prepared to write this book that I realized something very important. I did everything right as a parent to ensure the safety of my children. I made sure they were securely fastened in their seatbelts before I pulled out from that last gas station. I made sure they had sandwiches, coloring books, extra clothes, water, and snacks. We prayed before we left and always did a seatbelt check. What happened to my baby was an accident - and accidents do happen, to everyone and anyone I found my breath again after I accepted this fact. This wasn't just me, telling myself a version of the truth, because I verified it with the kids. They all assured me I did everything I normally do as a mom to ensure

I Never Dreamed You'd Leave in Summer

their safety. How could I ever doubt that?

Grief! Grief can blind you from the obvious and can consume you in a world of condemnation that is unbearable. Miscarriage, drowning, car accident, household accident, etc. Many misfortunes are accidental, NOT intentional. I am also aware that some things happen to children because we have made a bad judgement call, sometimes leading to loss of life. But I've learned that none of that matters when it comes to the redemptive plan of God through the cross of Jesus. I believe some of us have yet to fully understand the true message of salvation. I wonder sometimes, if we embraced the salvation of the cross and what it meant for us in this new covenant, how much more would we live in victory and peace? I knew this all this in my mind, but I had to embrace it with my heart for this part of my journey. If I live my life and expect to be rewarded solely based on what I did and didn't do, I was causing more suffering for myself. Romans 8:1 tells me if I am in Christ Jesus,

I don't live my life in a dreary conundrum, never coming to a place of completion in healing of the wounds in my soul. Christ Jesus gave me a way back to Him to redeem me. The enemy, in complete opposition, only comes to steal, kill, and destroy. Christ came to give us life in abundance. I believe that the life He came to give us is to be lived on earth and in eternity. Living that life on earth will put the enemy to shame and turn the heads of men in wonderment at the Father. Some may ridicule and acknowledge no place for redemption and grace, but that's the world we live in. Take everything good that God provides in your life right now and live from it. Let it fuel you and restore your zeal and zest for life. You're still here and the life you have is because of Him. You can't work hard enough to gain his love and redemption. He offers it freely for whomever will take it from Him.

I've encountered many circumstances and situations where and I've re-experienced the pain and loneliness I felt when my

I Never Dreamed You'd Leave in Summer

daughter was taken from me. In counseling, they call these times or events "triggers" because of the chain reaction of feelings or behaviors they elicit. I learned to recognize my triggers and stay away from people, places, and situations that would trigger the worst reactions. I eventually grasped the concept of turning my triggers into steps. Breaking down my triggers into manageable pieces or steps allowed me to gain control of them so that they changed my perspective on life and no longer kept me imprisoned. It wasn't just the death of my daughter that brought me here. These triggers would often be linked to childhood and early adulthood traumas. They were humps that I couldn't seem to get over and Symara's passing was the final straw. I knew this last trauma would either make me or break me. I was right there holding her when she slipped away. I was right there when she flew past me and I couldn't catch her. You can't just turn those memories off and forget. But I did decide to never, ever again, allow the enemy to take my trauma, tragedy, and hardships and use them against me. I decided to take my life back and throw the pain back in Satan's face. The pain that he inflicted on me brought me beyond human frailty. I was done letting him get the best part of me anymore. I had to take my life back and reclaim myself. I had to go and reclaim that little girl who was traumatized and forgotten. I had to go let that little girl out of prison and chains so I could heal from the rest of the adult issues that plagued me.

There's a back story to trauma and tragedy and we need to revisit those times, those issues so we can let that person we were then out of their bonds. For some people, just acknowledging that the trauma happened and you are still here, intact, that is the first step toward wholeness. Other people may just need to go face that giant with the sword of the spirit and cut off its head. There is an ultimate victory in your life journey no matter what route you take to move

I Never Dreamed You'd Leave in Summer

forward. Sometimes one pain triggers another. I know the death of my little girl resurrected some unresolved issues in my life. For instance, I was bullied as a child. It was ugly and so frequent, more than half of the time I didn't even tell my parents or a teacher when it did happen to me. When I'd had enough, I'd fight and that wasn't cute at all. When I would fight, I went for broke because in my mind, we were not going to have this conversation again. I dealt with people trying to intimidate me during the process of burying my daughter. Sometimes, I was just too devastated to fight back and other times I was just alert enough to fight back and win.

When we tried to retrieve Symara's social security number to get access to her life insurance policy we had a hard time. All the contents of my purse were scattered across the highway and important papers were left at home. Thankfully, Kevin's employer was able to get him to the right resources to get the paperwork started. We approached the woman at the customer service desk and we told her what we needed and why. She replied, "Well, do you have anything with your and her name on it?". I told her "No, we don't, we were on a trip and our daughter died and we need to bury her." The woman then replied, "I don't care what the situation was, if you don't have anything with her name on it, I can't help you." Kevin had taken my cane from next to me and leaned it on the wall next to him. When I asked him later why he did that, he said he thought that my emotional state would have pushed me to pick up my cane and clean off her desk with it. At the time, I didn't know he'd moved my cane but I can understand why.

Tragedy and death trigger emotions of anger, rage, pain, resentment, and stress. I went through them all - and went through them without involving others in my space. I wanted to grieve alone but there were times I wanted the company of someone who could just listen and not give me advice. I simply needed an ear to listen to me talk it out and I couldn't

I Never Dreamed You'd Leave in Summer

find anyone like that. People meant and mean well, but I didn't want to hear what I needed to do, I just wanted to cry. I didn't know who and how to trust anyone with that part of me. I have lived most of my life very open and transparent about mostly everything, but this part of my life was intimate and I didn't want to lay out in the open and bleed. Being able to talk openly about Symara's death and its impact on my life meant I had to risk trusting someone and that would not be easy to do. In fact, I hold fast to this painful part of my life's journey. It's more precious to me now than it's ever been, now that I can see the bigger picture.

Crystal P. Willingham

You can't really detach yourself from the emotion of a loss. It's impossible, because you're human.

Chapter 5
The Bigger Picture

How can we see or even begin to understand the bigger picutre you ask? In every low and high place in my life, there was always something more to be seen and understood. God works within the events of our lives in ways that are mysterious – in ways that we may only comprehend in hindsight. The Message bible says, "That's why we can be sure that every detail in our lives of love for God is worked into something good." (Romans 8:28) My husband defines this as the sovereignty of God. Our love for Him sets us up for an outcome that we can call good. An outcome that allows His glory to shine in the middle of something dark and tragic. He told Jeremiah (Jer. 29:11) He had plans for a hopeful future for him. If God had plans for me with a hopeful future and I'm only focused on my present pain, I'm going to miss what that hopeful future is all about. The crazy thing is, I forgot sometimes to look at all the pain in my life and ask what good could come from it, even though I had Jesus' example.

My pain and suffering are no different from any other human being on this planet. Someone can always relate to my pain but the glory of that pain is knowing it will all work together for our good. We don't just acknowledge God our creator, his son Jesus, and his presence known as Holy Spirit, we revere and love him, remembering He loved us first we when were just a thought in the mind of God. That's the kind

I Never Dreamed You'd Leave in Summer

of love that keeps you sane, focused, and driven to love others. I'm not a perfect human being. I have made, and will make, many mistakes in my life. Hopefully, there won't be any more life-altering mistakes but even in that, God's love conquers all, His grace abounds, and He is present in my life.

Death changes you. It changes your perspective on life and what life has to offer you. If you don't understand and embrace the concept of eternal life, death can and will change you in the most negative way possible. Although a person is gone from our lives, we can't think of their absence as something that will stop us from living forward. If you are still on this planet, a living breathing creature, then you are alive with purpose. As affirmed in the Bible (Ecclesiastes 3), there is a time to be born and a time to die. It is the inevitable cycle of life. I'm a believer or should I say, a follower of Christ Jesus and His teachings. I believe in eternal life through Him and that He is the passageway to God. To sum it up, I believe there is life after death and that life is with God if you choose to believe. My faith has kept me from allowing the aftermath of pain to destroy me. Death can change you but you have a choice as to how it changes you. You can let it teach you to appreciate life more, live it to the fullest in your faith, and trust God will be there for the rest of your life's journey. Or, you can let the death of a loved one destroy your faith and believe that God is a terrible higher power who can't possibly love you. You might think if he did love you he wouldn't have taken that person away from you. We never stop to think that God may have taken that person for that person's benefit. For instance, I am not certain that Symara would have enjoyed a good quality of life on earth after such an accident; what if she had been paralyzed or vegetative? Would my faith have been destroyed if my child had survived but been irreparably damaged? I do know that where she is now is so much more fulfilling to her than any life I would have given her on this planet. I would

I Never Dreamed You'd Leave in Summer

have loved to see her grow up and become the woman called Symara but that is not the case and never will be. I see her exit for what it has gifted me with. She was born, she saw, she conquered, and left me with the greatest gift of all; LOVE!

The love I have for myself has reached a new level while on this pathway. Love God, love yourself, and love your neighbor. How many times have I read that and didn't truly read it? I tried to love God for sure and love my neighbor, but I seemed to keep forgetting to love myself. When you don't love yourself, you tend to take whatever the enemy and life dishes out at you. You don't fight back and consider the fact that you are worth fighting for. The intensity that trauma brings will keep you focused on what you've lost and distract you from what remains. You may have lost someone, but you are still here and you just have to live forward in trust and faith.

Death changes your behavior - and the person who has died doesn't have to be a close friend, family member, spouse, or child to affect us. We have the power to choose how death impacts our lives. In my culture, as an African American woman raised in church, we embrace death in both sorrow and joy. We purposely sing songs that identify our sorrow and we use that song as an emotional outlet or release. Along with songs of sorrow, you can pretty much bank on some shouting, dancing and rejoicing for the life of the one who passed, and letting the ones left behind know one thing for sure, they are with the Lord. We don't miss a beat when it comes to a funeral. I am certain that a few of my friends and family are either chuckling as they read this, giving me an "umm hmm", or "I know that's right", as they reminisce on the many funerals we've participated in over the years. Funeral homes have adapted to unusual celebratory ways to help families deal with death. The hard-core reality of it all is this: after the homegoing celebration is over, after the gravesite has received new sod to cover the dirt, there is more grieving to be done.

I Never Dreamed You'd Leave in Summer

We empty homes and distribute memories to various family members to try to hold onto what is left of the life of the ones we miss. There's nothing wrong with memories and mementos - they have a place in our healing process. Familiarity does help us get through the early stages of grieving. We go to cemeteries and gravesites to try to make sense of how we feel. Mary Magdalene went to the tomb where Jesus was supposed to be "laid to rest" to keep a vigil there. She planned to be there for quite some time and grieve her Savior's death. She was standing vigil to grieve one of the greatest men of her time. The Savior of the world, the one who brought her dearly beloved brother Lazarus back from the dead after four days in the tomb. What a great and powerful person Jesus was to her. As she got there to set up camp, an angel of the Lord appeared to her and rolled the stone away from the tomb. Jesus was risen just like he said. Although we are talking about Jesus, we must understand there is a greater glory behind death that in our humanity we don't seem to embrace fully.

When you go to the gravesite of your loved one, you must realize they are not there, they have moved on to a greater glory. Now, as sons and daughters, we take on the task of remembering those that have gone on and take to heart the things that God has allowed them to do and be to us. Those are the treasures they left with us that fuel us to live forward. Don't miss that part! When Mary realized the greater glory in the death, burial, and resurrection of Jesus she got excited and took off running to tell the other disciples about what she had seen. I know, I know, you're probably saying, "Yeah, Crystal, that was Jesus the Christ. Where is the greater glory in the death of my loved one"? Remember earlier we talked about the sovereignty of God? All things work together for the good of those that love God and are called according to his purpose (Romans 8:28)? There is the greater glory. Even in death, God has a plan for this to work out for your good.

I Never Dreamed You'd Leave in Summer

Your next move is to *focus on the good in your life.* You have life inside of you, whether you have one friend, two, or many, there is someone rooting for you and praying for you. You can choose to see the light at the end of this sorrowful time or stay in the dark place. Staying in the dark place gives the enemy just the room he needs to destroy you and the lives of the people you may influence. It first begins with you and your choice to live freely in this life. Don't let the life of the person who once lived but is now gone be in vain. Take every bit of life wisdom, 'nuggets', and joys they gave you and plant them as seeds in your soul. Let those things turn into a harvest of joy, love, and peace. Embrace the memories, miss them, talk about them, and then get up and live what their life and death taught you.

As for me, how could I possibly live out the wisdom of a four-year-old girl? I have thought about this so many times and I've come up with so many answers. One life-altering tragedy turned into a life-changing moment that gives me a new perspective on life every single day. I learned how to not avoid the things that make me hurt, offend me, or cause me any sort of vexation. I tackle it head on - ok, well - most of them. I am the one who will open the can of worms and go fishing. I don't avoid things that remind me of that day, I keep living and I live through it. Symara died in August and by December, I was driving again. Nervous and shaking at every bump, pothole, crack in the street, and curve, but driving! I am still a little shaky at times, but I've learned to trust myself and trust anyone whose car I'm riding in. I use distractions like music, texting (ONLY if I'm not driving), and having normal conversation. Every now and again, I get jumpy when I see another driver isn't watching and we could end up in a fender bender. I'll never forget - I was out with someone a month after I got home from Detroit, I went to a church event on September 9, 2009 and while on the highway someone hit us. I

I Never Dreamed You'd Leave in Summer

was nervous and shaken up, but I got out of that car, walking cane and all, and walked right into that church. I felt empowered because I didn't let that fender bender cripple me and shut me down. I didn't give in to avoidance, I owned it, and conquered it. No, I didn't do that every single time because let's face it, I'm not perfect.

When bad memories would intrude on my space, I had to learn how to fight back. For instance, I had several dreams of that car flipping over on the highway. To this day, I can still remember the screams of my children and the look on every one of their faces as we turned over. I can remember every single detail of that moment. I can still remember the smell of scraped metal, gasoline, and shattered glass. Plenty of times those memories would intrude upon my peace at night and I'd wake up in a cold sweat looking for my children. This was textbook PTSD, but I never knew the term applied to me. I coped, at first, by dissociating myself from the memories and figuring out ways to shut off my painful emotions. I was hoping this would stop the night-time intrusion of memories and allow me to just ride it out. Sometimes I would long for affection from family or friends but it didn't come, so I learned to disconnect from my emotions so as not to feel hurt or tap into the emotions attached to that painful day. What I didn't realize was that I was cutting myself off from all positive feelings too, including love. In nearly every single possible way that love would show up, I ran from it. I started to convince myself that if I loved something or someone, I would lose them or it. I wasn't paying attention to what and who was around me, not being mindful. When I realized I wasn't appreciating and embracing what God was bringing into my space such as His peace, joy, stillness, and healing I had to shift my thinking. I realized I hadn't acknowledged that the rest of my children walked away with barely a scratch on them. I forgot when I looked up at my five-month-old son, he was smiling at me. I forgot my oldest daughter got out of that truck speaking in tongues and giving God the praise even though she knew we were in bad shape. I forgot how many x-rays they took looking for what should have been wrong with me. I was told when I was discharged that they did find bleeding on my brain and I needed to have some therapy. I forgot how many people's lives were changed because of Symara's passage into glory. I began to remember and think on these things like instructed in Philippians 4:8. Think about the things around you that are true, honest, pure, and good. Redirect your focus when you become deadlocked in toxic grief as though you are spiraling down a black hole. Will you forget sometimes? Oh yes - you will surely forget but eventually this will become so much a part of you that you'll hear the Holy Spirit speak through you and through other channels to remind you of Whose you are. Don't let yourself or the enemy erase or throw paint on the bigger picture; the testament of His glory coming through for and in you. Don't do what I did and isolate yourself; isolation is the enemy's trap and prison for your life. He will use any circumstance to bring you away from the fold instead of toward it. The words of King Solomon in Proverbs 11:14 says, "Without good direction, people lose their way; the more wise counsel you follow, the better your chances." Stay connected to the right people – go in search of the right people if you have to, who can hear your story and help guide you through to a better outlook on your life.

Find new ways to express yourself. Pick up a new hobby, jump on a plane and go somewhere you've always wanted to go, or do something you've never done before, but always wanted to do. Be intentional and engage in life activities to keep you aware of what is in the world around you. Give back to your community and let others see the light of His glory as you help others. Remember, the power to choose in your

I Never Dreamed You'd Leave in Summer

hands. You can be intentional in walking through the process of grief. How do I know this? Some things I never read about or studied; I just knew it. Somehow, circumstances in my life taught me to be resilient and I didn't even know it. I started to journal a little here and there. I even started a blog, which has since been taken down, but all the same I did things to keep me alive and actively participating in the life I was and am still living.

Crystal P. Willingham

Chapter 6
What Next?

One thing I am certain about is this: Your walk with God reveals that you have the power to push forward through the grieving. You just need to be reminded of who you are in Jesus. You need to keep hearing it until you snap back. Learn how to take some time out for yourself and relax. Go away from the noise and be alone with yourself and with God. Speak to him and listen for him to speak back to you.

God doesn't always respond to us audibly. I've literally sat down at times and asked God to come visit with me and the wind would blow over my face and his peace would fall on me like a layer of skin. Several times I'd be sitting somewhere and a yellow butterfly would flutter past me. When Symara crossed over we saw yellow butterflies everywhere. When I'm feeling extra blue and I miss her a little more than usual, yellow butterflies would find me and land very, very close by me. I knew then that God was letting me know that He knows how I feel and how much I miss her. Most of the time when they pop up, I'm with someone who knows my story very well and they embrace that moment with me. I learned to be intentional in how I share it.

I'll emphasize Philippians 4:8 for reminding you of the purposes of meditating on the things around you that God himself intentionally placed in your ecosystem. Music played a big role in my times of meditation, prayer, and the word of

I Never Dreamed You'd Leave in Summer

God. Find the kind of music that resonates with what you are looking for. His love, His peace, which is ultimately His presence. I've even gone so far as to play the Bible on mp3 in my earbuds at night. This was how I was able to shake those intrusive moments when remembered trauma tried to overtake my peaceful sleep. I began to say to myself, I am His beloved and He will give me sweet rest; I learned this technique as a child, when I used to have recurring nightmares. I heard someone say they learned to call Jesus in their sleep. I resolved in my mind that I would not have that nightmare anymore and taught myself how to wake up by thinking on Jesus. In my dreams something would cover my mouth so I couldn't yell out. But you better believe my mind was working right! I'd think my way out until I was close enough to being awake that I could say the name of Jesus.

Stay connected to your support system whether that be your church, family, friends, co-workers, etc. Keep in mind that each group will support you in different ways so it's not fair to expect the intimacy of support from a co-worker that your family gives you. If you find yourself in a situation where you need more intimate support, then make sure you are intentional in reaching out to those that can. Press through those times when you may feel like your emotions are out of control. Generally speaking, suppressing your emotions can lead to their unhealthy expression, such as physical illness or negative impacts to relationships.

One reason you may be controlling your feelings is because you haven't found a healthy or safe outlet to release them. There are a variety of healthy outlets such as talking to a counselor or therapist, journaling, writing poetry, novels, painting, dancing, or singing. There are many creative ways to express your feeling and release your emotions, some may be unique to you. If you don't look for or discover ways to release your emotions in constructive ways, they may erupt in other

I Never Dreamed You'd Leave in Summer

ways and at times you least expect it. When I'm having a day where I miss my little girl, I say so to my family. If I'm feeling condemnation for her death, it's normally right at the time something wonderful is about to happen to me and my focus gets diverted from the good that is happening or about to happen. Recognize those moments so you'll know which ones to own and which ones to push out of your space. The moments you own are the ones you embrace for the very purpose of healing you. You are human, and you'll feel the loss of someone's passing often. The tough moments that come as a distraction, the ones that divert you form your purpose, the ones that originate with the enemy, let them go and push past them.

Finally, take control of your life. You can say what you want to participate in and what you don't. There are three occasions that bring out the best and worst in people: weddings, births, and funerals. Without bringing harm to anyone, I have to say that some family members were pretty ugly towards me after the accident. I forgave them and their thoughts and deeds are between them and God. You must forgive others, and do so swiftly, or what they did to you will eat away at your soul. That's not good for the healing process at all. Choose your battles and speak up when you need to. Don't let anyone bring shame and condemnation to you as a result of the death of your loved one. I will speak specifically to parents about this one. Yes, we are supposed to love, cherish and protect our babies. However; human error is a beast when it comes to children. I watched a documentary recently where several couples whose children had died were interviewed. The death of their child was a result of them leaving the child in the car. Every parent either thought the other parent took care of the child or they simply forgot the baby was in the car. How could you forget your baby was in the car? I can't answer that. As I watched the program, hearing and seeing what this mistake did to each parent, I can surely say there is no punishment worse than the pain you'd feel after making a mistake like that. Humans err – frequently, and humans can be bullies when it comes to someone else's mistake. It seems that we can too easily find ourselves in a glass house, with someone only too willing to throw stones at us. You don't have to accept what others are saying, but you do have to accept what you say to yourself. Speak positivity into your own life until those words impact your mind toward positive change. You will never be the same again. What you experienced in this loss has changed you forever. But you can choose how it changes you. Will it be for the better or for the worse? Don't ever let anyone tell you, or don't ever tell yourself, that you don't deserve to move on with your life and find joy in living it to the fullest, the way God intended. Jesus came down to earth, not only to give you passageway to the Heavenly Father through Him but to give you the best He has for your earthly and eternal life.

Symara left my life suddenly but God made sure I was prepared for it all along. There are still times that I remember her, and my heart feels the pain of her absence. There was one thing I promised myself, even though I had times where I didn't feel the will to live that I have been able to keep., That promise was for me to keep living and not let Symara's passage to glory go by unnoticed. If that meant exposing my pain and being vulnerable so others can heal, then so be it. If that meant letting relationships go, then so be it. Symara's passing wasn't the only thing I lived through, but it was the last thing I lived through that I was going to let rob me of what God sustained me for. God didn't leave me here to suffer, He left me here because he anointed me to speak good news, His love for humanity. He called me to bring healing to the heartbroken people. He called me to herald people in captivity the message of freedom. He sent me to show you how His grace is working in your life. God really turned my mourning

I Never Dreamed You'd Leave in Summer

into morning.

Crystal P. Willingham

Chapter 7
Trauma

Apostle Marlon Willingham

Conversations on trauma prevail today more than any other time we've known. Identifying trauma and the impact it has across various people groups, socioeconomic groups, genders and more has evolved to include a myriad of vulnerable people subject to experiencing trauma. Clinicians in the field of trauma determine its definition to be experiencing an overwhelming event that an individual unexpectedly endures, creating a psychological insult that impose life-threatening thoughts towards self or others. Composed within this view of trauma lies perception. Not all events are traumatic for everyone, relevance is meaningful as to how a person understands the event; however, when a traumatic event occurs, regardless how severe or mild it may seem to others, ultimately, the individual's internal meaning about the event is central to their overall experience.

Understanding what trauma does is key for not only the individual but also for those who may love and care about that individual. Once traumatized by a life experience, there are many symptoms that will occur, typically immediately after the traumatization. A common misconception by most is that nothing is wrong with the person because maybe they go back to work quickly, or they seem to be okay because they are smiling or joking again. Many times, old behaviors that seem to continue as normal are not accurate signals that a traumatized individual is okay. Here are some important insights when understanding how trauma impact the psychological, physiological, and emotional construct.

Psychologically, we all may know someone that has had such an experience that traumatized them. This individual probably demonstrated psychological trauma in ways that were very obviously or not so obvious. Maybe they developed amnesia, loss of memory about details of the event. Some may have trouble talking about their experience therefore choosing to avoid any conversation regarding that experience. Those who are grieving from the loss of a loved one to sudden death from an accident or an unanticipated event will say things like, "I'll just not think about it anymore." Grief, like most trauma outcomes, is typically accompanied by invading thoughts of the traumatic episodes during the darkness of night while asleep. Dreams become a place where re-experiencing the event intrudes upon their sleep and even cause insomnia, night sweats, and semi-conscious sleep patterns. Let us not forget about daytime images that flash in the mind of those who grieve. These images haunt the person during the day with unwanted images of their experience. The psychological effect trauma has on a person is devastating enough to cause decision-making ability to be impaired; illogical choices that are harmful are made. When grief is involved, sufferers battle with self-blame, suicidal thoughts, and condemnation. Their view of the world changes and their view of themselves becomes distorted. Lamenting extended beyond a reasonable period-of-time will develop into a form of depression causing impairment in social engagement, marital health and intimacy, and without proper support could lead to a debilitating lifestyle of mental alteration.

Physiological effects of trauma inflicted on a person can

cause chronic suffering. Those who suffer from sexual abuse may experience pelvic pain, abdominal pain or other such pain in their lower region. Obviously, depending on the experience sufferers will indicate different sorts of physiological issues. There are some trauma experiences that cause sufferers to develop curvature of the spine. Others may endure headaches or migraines. These types of symptoms can be found among those who experience car crashes for example. Also, from a biological perspective, trauma victims may suffer from uncontrollable twitching (tics). Issues with a person's respiratory system could become shallowed or hyper during perceived post trauma threat. Stress responses become hyper and chronic which increase vulnerability for diabetes, cardiovascular disease and chronic fatigue. Grief ridden persons will cry often for seemingly no reason. Also, sufferers of grief at times will have somatic physiological pain that does not really exist.

Emotional survivors of trauma are adversely influenced causing at times emotional upheaval. The inner emotional scar that trauma victims silently carry seeks to rob them of experiencing a whole and well-balanced life. There are so many ways in which emotionally imbalanced trauma sufferers endure that attempting to stop the emotional pain can only be resolved by turning to external coping resources (e.g., alcohol, sex, drugs, food). Here's what must be understood about the emotional scarring that comes with trauma: "Just because I'm not crying doesn't mean I'm not hurting." Repressing emotional pain is counter-productive for the individual and for those who will have a meaningful relationship with that person. One thing for sure, although escaping the pain by not thinking about it may seem best, however, the pain is still there. After years of repressing the pain of losing an unborn child to a car accident, my client sat in my office holding back the tears of losing a child. It was clear in that moment that the decision to move on was not the right decision. It was now time to work on the emotional pain. Grief is certainly an emotional response to a traumatic life event. Those suffering with grief may exhibit mood swings, irritability at small things, depressive episodes (feeling down for periods of time), disconnect from others (e.g., spouse, family), unable to verbally connect their emotions with words, emotionally flat (stoic), or sexually disconnected.

Someone may be wondering, how does a person overcome trauma? Unfortunately, addressing the "how" takes more time than what can be written here, but there are some very vital insights related to overcoming the effects of trauma that can be shared. First, begin by researching therapists that are trauma informed. That simply means, make sure your counselor understands the dynamics of trauma and can assist you via that framework. Second, prepare yourself to enter counseling open to the experience and vulnerable in exposing your past and daily experience. Third, build a support system. Your support system may or may not be your family members. It is Okay! Supporters are those that do one thing, Support You! If you are saying I don't have any or I just have one, that's all you need and look at those around you who may not seem that obvious. Here's a fact. Those who have a good support system are more likely to recover from trauma and experience a reduction in its impact. Fourth, be patient with the process. There will be moments of reliving the trauma during counseling and outside of counseling. As you continue to work with a qualified therapist you will find a reduction in symptoms. Fifth, find time to incorporate prayer and meditation into your work. Receiving strength from the Father of Heaven through our Lord and Savior Jesus Christ is a great benefit we have as His children. I pray you or your loved one finds the peace that surpasses all understanding as you seek a victorious journey beyond the grief of trauma, God bless.

I Never Dreamed You'd Leave in Summer

Marlon B. Willingham has a bachelor's degree in business and a master's degree in clinical and mental health counseling from Liberty University.

Marlon is currently in his doctoral studies and will be complete in Summer 2020

About the Author

Crystal Willingham is married to Marlon, mother of 5; Chelcie (Deathony) Diamon, Sydnie, & Kevin Jr. and grandmother to Symara Chanel Rose. She is currently presiding in Columbia, SC. She is the owner of Clear as Crystal Entertainment LLC est. in 2007. She is the founder of "HeySis" an online women's empowerment organization. Crystal was ordained in the ministry in 1999, affirmed as a prophet & apostle in 2005.

Crystal travels from time to time to speak to women's groups, in churches, and other platforms about her story and how it has changed her life. Her live and in color presentation is far more deepening and soul rescuing than her book. Crystal gives all the honor to God, her family, and the love and care of her friends that pushed her to healing on this journey. You can follow her on all social media @iamclearascrystal or contact her on her website

www.iamclearascrystal.com

Acknowledgments

This book is dedicated to my four remaining children Chelcie, Diamond, Sydnie, & Kevin Jr. I love you so much more than I could ever say.

To the first responders on I-75 in Jellico, Tennessee at 9:15pm on August 13, 2009. The beautiful angels on staff at UT Medical Center and the social workers of Campbell County Tennessee. Ellis & Ellis Funeral Home, Apostolic Faith Temple, One Accord Ministries International, and Soul Harvest Ministries of Detroit, Michigan.

The family of Kevin Smith Sr. Symara's father. You are her grandmother, aunts, uncles, cousins, and friends. My family, the Davis' & Barge families, thank you for what you did for me in this extremely hard time.

My Atlanta, GA family, thank you for keeping my head above water.

Marlon, my forever love, what can I say on these pages that won't *take me the rest of my life to complete. You are my best friend, my heart, and my wise counsel. I couldn't have prayed for you if I tried.*

In Memory of:

Doris Lorene Davis
Calvin Davis Sr.
Bertha Smith
Keith Smith
Margaret Smith
Richard Hill Sr.
Richard Hill Jr.
Jerrod Hill Jr.
Deante Cross Benson

www.ingramcontent.com/pod-product-compliance
Lightning Source LLC
Chambersburg PA
CBHW031321160426
43196CB00007B/616